Understanding Ascension
The Sacred Science of Ascension Mechanics

Saira Salmon

Pathways to Consciousness

© Saira Salmon 2024. All rights reserved

No part of this publication may be reproduced in any way without the written permission of the author. All warranties, express or implied are disclaimed. Neither publisher nor author is liable for any damages, including consequential damages, that may result from the use of this information. There is no perceived slight of any individual or organisation intended, just expression of the author's sincerely held beliefs.

This edition: 2024

ISBN: 9798303592605
Imprint: Future Perfect Publishing

Website: www.sairasalmon.com
Facebook: Saira Salmon
YouTube: Saira Salmon

Available as an e-book

Other Books by the Author:

Understanding Starseeds – *Discover Your Galactic Origins & Soul Frequency to Awaken the Eternal Divine Human Within*
Complete Chakras – *Understand Their Importance and Master their Power to Transform Your Life*
Your Goddess Archetypes – *Align & Master Your Feminine Creative Power and the Archetypal Forces Within to Transform Your Life & Relationships*
Grail Wisdom – *Understanding the Multitude of Energies that Make Up the Many Layers of the Web of Life in the Third Dimension*

Pathways to Consciousness Series:
*The **Pathways to Consciousness** series of booklets seeks to explore and outline a series of basic principles and concepts any aspiring metaphysician or wisdom- seeker requires as a foundational base of knowledge in their studies.*

The Wheel of Life - *the Powerful Energetic Archetype that Attunes Us to the Rhythms & Flows of Natural Cycles*
The Universal Laws – *Beyond the Law of Attraction. Understand & Harmonise with the Cosmic Forces of Creation to Live a Life of Meaning & Purpose*
The Four Elements & Elemental Energy - *A Beginner's Guide to Understanding the Subtle Forces that Underpin Manifest Creation*
Understanding Ascension – *The Sacred Science of Ascension Mechanics*

Contents

FOREWORD 11

INTRODUCTION – THE BIG PICTURE 13

WHAT IS ASCENSION? 31

MULTIDIMENSIONALITY BASICS 41

MULTIDIMENSIONAL EARTH 48

MULTIDIMENSIONAL DNA 51

MULTIDIMENSIONAL SELF OR STATIONS OF IDENTITY 55

ASCENSION STAGES 59

THE DIFFERENT PATHS BACK TO SOURCE 65

FALSE SACRED SCIENCE TEACHINGS 73

OTHER BLOCKS TO ASCENSION 83

THE ROLE OF STARSEEDS, INDIGOS AND LIGHTWORKERS ... 91

OUR JOURNEY TO 5D 97

PERSONAL AND PLANETARY CHAKRA CHANGES 105

THE AURORA RACES 111

BIFURCATION OF TIMELINES 115

CHRISTOS LAW OF ONE TEACHINGS 119

SUMMARY 125

APPENDIX A THE DIFFERENCE BETWEEN FIBONACCI V KRYSTAL SPIRALS 133

APPENDIX B – THE CDT PLATES 140

APPENDIX C - THE NET AND FREQUENCY FENCES 145

ABOUT SAIRA AND HER WORK 151

ACKNOWLEDGMENTS 153

Dedication:
To Lisa Renee
whom I have neither met nor spoken to, but consider a valued mentor. As information from the consciousness fields was pouring into my awareness and had me wondering if I had wandered into an alternative reality, connecting to her body of work anchored me in my own inner gnosis and enabled me to join lots of dots.
Thank you!

Foreword

For many years it has been clear to me that there is a lost science of ascension teachings. It wasn't just a 'mystical' path, or a spiritual one, but a clearly laid out and understood process.

It was obviously taught in the early Egyptian temples – and had just as obviously been corrupted by the latter part of Ancient Egyptian history. I caught glimpses of it in what little we know of Bardic/Druidic teachings, as well as early Christian and Gnostic writings and came to understand that this Sacred Science was taught widely within the high civilisations of Atlantis and those that came before.

So much has been deliberately obfuscated, corrupted, twisted and warped that it has been difficult to find the thread of resonant truth that is still there, and in the many years I have searched to understand what this 'science' was I have been up lots of dead ends.

But finally, little-by-little a picture began to emerge from the mist. I found the right threads to pull on and what emerged both validated that early 'knowing' I had pursued, and stunned me at the level of misdirection that was being taught in some of the more mainstream teachings I had studied.

I had to unlearn much of what I had been taught, by well-meaning and sincere teachers, and what I came to understand changed the way I fundamentally view _everything_. In a good way! Although it is very difficult, initially, to find yourself on shifting sands, the process of having to construct firm foundations based on a totally different understanding of who we truly are, our untold history and origins, have been so affirming, so horizon-expanding it has been like reclaiming a lost part of myself.

And, indeed, humanity has been lost to itself, deliberately deprived of its true history, a true understanding of its purpose and potential, by those who see us as little more than farm animals, enslaved and harvested for their own negative purposes.

Did you come here to be a wage slave, pay taxes and work yourself to a standstill? No, you have a bigger purpose and vision than that. I hope, by laying out my current understanding of why your Soul chose to incarnate here, and the processes we have to engage with to begin the organic ascension journey back to wholeness that it will trigger some remembering in you of who you *truly* are, and why you are *truly* here.

Saira

Introduction – The Big Picture

Let's begin by looking at the big concepts that form a back drop to our reality and what is going on. In the process I shall introduce you to various concepts which you are likely unfamiliar with. Take heart – if it does not make sense to you now, the more you come back to this, the more will slot into place. None of this information is taught to us by our parents, our education system or our religious teachers, so we are starting with an almost clean sheet and having to build anew our understanding.

Probably the most important thing for us to be clear on as we find our way onto the Ascension path is that ALL life-forms and beings[1] are Source Embodied. Everything has come from Source and is a part of Source. It has never been necessary to go outside of your own innate Source connection for anything, whether it be healing, assistance, knowledge etc. All of this is available to you through your Source connection, and working to strengthen this on a daily basis is the best work you can do to help yourself.

We have been taught, and come to believe, otherwise. We give our power to so-called 'experts' who mislead, misdirect and misinform us against what is right for you, the individual, unique spark of the Divine that you are, that carries all that it needs within it.

When it comes to healing, true healing, it is ultimately the energy of Source that is the only thing that can heal what is not working correctly within any life-form or being. If there are sufficient levels of Source energy flowing into a being, then everything will be working correctly, so if something is not working correctly then

---

[1] When I refer to life forms and beings I mean any form of consciousness, which goes from other humans, animals etc to planetary systems, solar systems, star systems and even galaxies. Consciousness is apparent in many forms.

it is as a result of being insufficient energy from Source being able to flow to and into the life-form.

Why might this be? Every life-form or being is built on an energy template which is designed to hold high levels of Source energy. If it is unable to do this it is because the template has become distorted or damaged in some way. For thousands of years now the template or blueprint of all life on Earth has been damaged due to what has been unfolding here during this last Dark Age[2].

My hope is that by the time you have finished reading this book you will have some understanding of the steps you can take to change this.

When it comes to healing the reality is that only YOU can heal yourself, no other person can heal you, only facilitate. Healing requires your active participation and another can guide and help you, but not do it on your behalf. Let us be really clear about this, because so many hand over responsibility for their healing to others. The healing impulse MUST come from within, via your Source connection. It is a free will choice to engage with this healing Source energy, and if you will take no responsibility for the process, let alone any engagement with it any 'healing' received is at best superficial.

No Krystic being – and by this I mean someone who follows the Christos teaching of unity consciousness and the Law of One which we will look at later - will <u>ever</u> interfere or intervene in another's free will choice, and this includes forcing healing energy against another's wishes. If at the higher Self level the being is not choosing to heal (maybe because there is a life lesson still to learn?) then any healing energy given will be deflected rather than absorbed.

---

[2] This began around 26,000 years ago, and was accelerated with the final fall of the civilisation of Atlantis.

Once we are able to clearly re-establish a strong Source connection and can start to access the higher frequency levels this permits, we can begin to experience many things that have not been available on this planet for many aeons.

As ever-higher levels of Source energy begin to flow once again we can begin to 'remember' that we are part of a multi-dimensional family of consciousness that exists within our personal connection to Source. They are US existing at a higher dimensional level within creation, an integral part of the wholeness of who we are. Thus, as part of US we should have open communication with this 'family' at ALL times. It is a sign of the damage we have sustained that we do not.

In order to heal those aspects of us that are not working correctly or as they should, we have to work to connect to the higher frequency bands *above* the lower frequency bands that need healing, and draw these energies down into the lower bands. So, for example, if we are looking to heal 4th dimensional damage we will do this by drawing 5th dimensional frequency down into the 4th dimensional layers. Sound complicated doesn't it, but the body's innate wisdom knows how to do this if it has the right conditions.

It is vital we come to understand energy – where it comes from, where it goes, what we do with our energy, who we allow access to it, the effects this has and how we interact with energy ALL the time, at every level.

Co-Creation

The process of learning how to gain control over our own personal energy field and establishing how to consciously co-create our desired experience here is an essential part of our journey. In understanding this we begin to understand the co-creative partnerships we have at various levels and how our energy interacts continuously in acts of co-creation either at the level of mass consciousness at a planet-wide level or within our own personal reality.

When it comes to healing, our own desire for healing is a reflection of the desire of Source to heal ALL of itself ie. this Creation. Despite this, there may well still be parts that are not yet ready, or do not want to allow healing and we must understand that Source is okay with this, as it has given every aspect of this Creation a free will choice as to whether to participate or not in what is offered unconditionally.

There are many life-forms or beings within our Time Matrix which have reached a level of sickness and digression beyond the point of being able to hold the Source energy required to heal. It has been their choice to reach this state, and yet despite this, they are all loved by Source and are a part of the whole. We would refer to this as a Fallen life-form or being. It is important we understand that Source loves all of its Creation, fallen or otherwise. If a part does not want to heal Source does not force any part to accept the healing flows of Source energy that are being sent into any damaged system should the individual reject this.

Those beings whose template is damaged beyond their ability to heal still *need* Source energy though, in order to exist, despite the fact they can no longer receive it due to the levels of damage they have chosen to sustain, and are not desirous of doing what is required to re-establish a Source connection. It is a conundrum which these beings solve by *stealing* the necessary energy from other life-forms which still have the ability to receive Source energy.

These energy parasites drive all the wars and struggles within this system. All the conflicts down through the aeons have all been over energy – who owns it, who uses it etc.

Any life-form or being, be it biological, planetary, universal or even galactic, can only hold as much Source energy as the capacity of its template allows. Should it try to take in and run more energy than its system can hold then it would overload, blow up and shatter. It is not just a question of zapping a load of high frequency energy into a being. If there is damage in the templating at any level it can be problematic. Source will only send into a system the amount of energy that can safely be taken.

To enable higher levels of Source energy into a damaged template a 'spark' of Source is sent into any system that requires this and desires healing. These 'sparks' embody, encase, surround, merge with and become part of the system or life-form wanting healing.

We are ALL sparks of Divine Source and come into a system in order to take on and transform what requires healing by working to embody more of the energy of Source within whatever life-form or consciousness structure we inhabit. You may not have thought of your purpose here at this level, but it is an aspect all of us take on when we choose to incarnate our consciousness into a damaged system and body template – and Earth *is* damaged.

Those beings that are damaged beyond being able to embody Source energy have come about as a result of ignorance, of being unable to remember the truth of who they are. They have forgotten the Divine Spark they hold within. We call those who no longer have the ability – or desire - to heal their template Fallen Angelics, Fallen Races, Negative Beings, Black Hole entities and a variety of other names.

All the numerous wars, conflicts, struggles and agendas within this system have ultimately been over energy and who controls it, who uses it, who steals it and from whom, who gives it away through ignorance or coercion and so on. It is a precious resource for those who only have access to finite levels of energy.

These conflicts are a direct result of those who chose **not** to heal their template still wanting eternal life[3]. Their means of maintaining this (at least whilst others are available to 'feed' off) is to become parasites. So they maintain the illusion of eternal life, when in reality this is only possible due to stealing another's life force. This is where logic fails you because, in order to be immortal and become 'gods' they actually made a choice to be finite and can only maintain their 'immortality' by sucking the energy from all living matrices.

Trapped in Time

Within the many consciousness grids that make up a planet, solar or universal system there are many specific energetic points of connection where Source energy flows through in a concentrated form to disperse into the greater levels of the system, and all wars have been 'grid wars' in this context for control of these powerful energetic points. Our forebears were well aware of these places. They are the nodes, power-points, vortexes and places of power we are rediscovering.

When a system and its life-forms are unable to receive the required amount of Source energy to heal they become what is called 'trapped in time'. Being unable to hold sufficient frequency there is an inability to ascend into the higher dimensional reality fields of the system and return to unity with Source, to become one with ALL creation once more.

Those parts of Source, the life-forms that WANT to heal and make this return to Source will seek to heal all those parts of itself that desire to be free. This is the process we are seeing underway here at this time as a mass wave of Source energy helps lift personal and mass consciousness on this planet to the point where this healing wave of energy is lifting the planet and all the life-forms wanting to participate beyond the level of access of

---

[3] Never forget our divine template is eternal, a fact we have lost sight of in our short-lived earth bodies.

those with Fallen consciousness and their continual battleground for energy control.

Those who do not wish to participate will eventually lose access to their Source 'batteries' and begin to parasitize off each other, until the finite energy quanta of each resource is fully exhausted. They WILL return to Source, but it will not be through the ascension pathway, but rather a descension path, one that is called Space Dust Return or Space Dust Fragmentation Return. They are a part of Source, and when their finite energy is spent and they cannot vampirise off anything else they will go through the organic death process and return to Source.

The damage that has been done to our Sun by the destructive manipulations of the Fallen Races, for example, has gone beyond a point where it can be healed or reversed to enable our Sun, Sol, to become ascension-able once more (Our Sun holds a universal gate system). It still has many billions of years of energy quanta left and will go through its organic death cycle through this time, continuing to support this system whilst it can do so. Once it reaches the end of this process, it too will be able to return to Source, it just will not be through the ascension process. This is just one example of many where the actions of the Fallen Angelics have overridden and been destructive to the free will choices of others.

Krystal River Host and Krystal Spiral

Those wishing to participate in the normal ascension processes for many thousands of years have been prevented from doing so due to the extensive levels of damage which have been inflicted on the various gate systems at different levels of the multi-dimensional universe. This has been part of the Fallen Angelics attempt to prevent their 'batteries' from escaping their control. The normal ascension process of receiving high frequency Source energy coming down through successive levels of gates cannot be followed without a very real risk of overload and explosion due to the damage many of these gates have sustained.

When this became apparent, at the start of this Ascension cycle, something called the Krystal River Host was put in place, where the extra-dimensional races of the Krystal River Host[4] opened up their gate connections into our Time Matrix from their neighbouring Universe and routed Source energy through to us this way to ensure running energy through damaged gates (and exploding them) could be avoided.

This enabled higher Source frequencies to slowly start to accrete and open up alternative ascension pathways for those life-forms and beings wanting to participate.

The Krystal, or Christos, energy is a direct Source energy current, of what might be called life-force, prana or chi. It is the route Source energy takes as it comes down through various levels into our Creation, and this is also the route our consciousness will take as it slowly ascends, level by level, in its expansion back to Source. It is an organic creation current.

The Fibonacci Spiral – also called the Fib-of-no-chi for reasons that will become obvious – is an inorganic creation spiral that consumes everything in its path in order to expand and has been put in place and is accessed by those unable to hold Source energy within themselves. It is the ultimate consumer model if you will, and is mentioned in many New Age teachings, particularly with regards to Sacred Geometry.

One spiral has infinite access to energy, whilst the other eventually consumes all that is in its unfolding path. One is eternal, the other finite.

In theory, it is a free will choice which energy current we can choose to follow, the reality is that here on Earth for many

---

[4] The Krystal River Host are from AqualaSha Galaxy, one of the God Worlds in the Seven Higher Heavens, a neighbouring Time Matrix to ours. They are also part of and work with the Aurora races

thousands of years there has been NO access to the Krystal current, until recently. That has meant that everything has had no choice but to develop according to the constraints of the Fibonacci spiral energy. All life on Earth has been captured into this.

A fallen reality field or life-form occurs when the Divine Template (also called the Kathara Grid or 12 Tree Grid) has sustained a crucial level of mass damage such that it no longer allows the template to hold the ability to receive the eternal life-sustaining energy of Source.

What we have been seeing in this part of the galaxy and within our own system is that Fallen races have banded together and joined forces in order to combine their reversed, distorted resources and energy supply in an effort to manipulate Earth (and other planets under similar attack) into a reverse spin. This would then bring Earth into alignment with the gate connections into their fallen black hole systems and enable them to drag Earth wholly into their black hole system, a process called Phantom Fall, where Earth and her many lifeforms would serve their energy needs for a long time to come, living in a version of Earth called Phantom or Shadow Earth, the ultimate fallen 'matrix'.

It was essential that Earth manage to sustain a certain level of frequency and energy in order to prevent this. Otherwise they would have been successful in accomplishing their aim. Remember however, Source desires to heal itself and has many mechanisms for allowing this healing to occur for those wishing it.

It is worth making the point here that a Krystic being *does not* fight; they simply stand and run the energy of Source to establish ever higher levels of protection or, if the need arises, they will simply find a means to move themselves out of the line of attack if possible. The Krystic Avatar Jesus talked of 'turning the other cheek'. It is a question of not meeting violence with violence, but moving around it, beyond it, avoiding it in any way possible. Otherwise you become what you fight.

It is not an easy path, and requires ingenuity at time to find ways round things. It also requires disciplines, no ego and clear focus on higher energy and purpose.

Because the Krystic Races of the Krystic River Host assisted Earth and her life-forms by establishing a mechanism to supply the higher flows of Source energy through their gate networks required to prevent Phantom Fall, it ensured Earth's energy field were sustained at a high enough level of energy accretion, despite the Fallen Races trying to steal and drain that energy to force Earth to drop its energy frequency. This has ensured that Earth was able to continue to rise and move itself along the higher energy path of the Krystal Spiral.

Consciousness either chooses the expansive path of Krystal Spiral or the contractive path of the Fibonacci Spiral, the inorganic creation spiral whose only method of expansion is to consume everything in its path.

End of the Grid Wars

We saw the end of the Grid Wars within our Time Matrix occur around the date of May 2012. It was at this time that the Earth and her life-forms were assisted to continue to rise higher in energy, following the path of the Krystal Spiral. There is a point where the two spirals intersect (see diagram) and this was the point of no return for the Fallen Angelics. They had no choice at this point but to split off and follow the Fibonacci flow of energy as they are unable to hold the higher energies of the Krystal spiral. Their template will not allow them to continue to rise into higher energies. All those whose template is able to hold the higher energies were assisted to

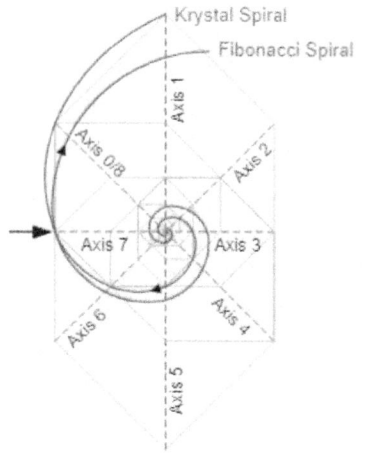

continue to follow the Krystal spiral flows.

The point of this 'split' occurring brought an instant end to the grid wars. The memo is working its way down the ranks to the various levels of minions tasked with 'making things happen' to ensure a steady supply of energy is fed to the Fallen races various energy harvesting mechanisms, who are in various stages of panic as very little they seem to do is bringing the desired results.

This process of the 'split' is referred to as the 'Bifurcation of Timelines' as the two groups – fallen and ascending – start to move ever further apart of their different evolutionary paths. Earth and her life-forms are now moving out of the reach of Fallen life-forms as they continue to accrete more and more Higher Source energy and the frequency gap between the two timelines begins to open ever wider.

2012 The End Times? No, a New Beginning

Many people on Earth were (mis)led to believe that on December 21 2012 Earth would move into a different dimensional reality with an enormous number of predictions about what this meant.

What actually occurred on December 21st 2012 was a stellar alignment whereby the stellar gates, or universal stargates, of our Time Matrix expanding up through the ever-higher dimensional frequency bands were brought into alignment.

This, coupled together with the fact that Earth was beginning to be able to hold more Source energy enabled the final three of what are called the Reuche Pillars[5] to be received and anchored into Earth's fields. Also called Override Pillars there are 12 Reuche Pillars in total and they originate in the highest levels of

---

[5] These energetic pillars are designed to correct energy currents to run photonic and sonic healing frequencies that amplify and power up the Krystal/Christos blueprint throughout the planet.

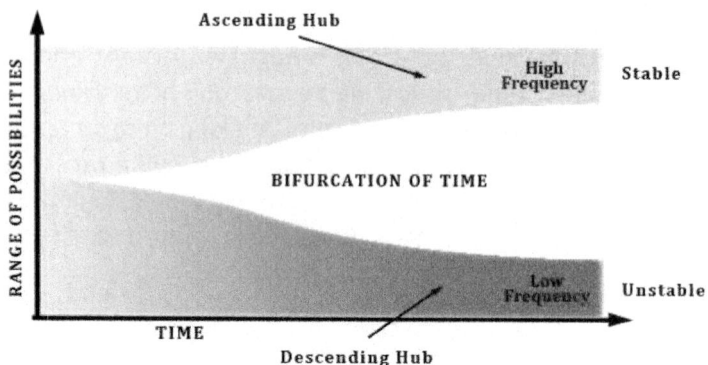

the Divine Blueprint, bringing the energies of this down into this density. The Reuche is the organic Divine Blueprint of First Creation of pure Source Consciousness ie. the original pure creation template.

Once anchored they are designed to correct any distortions in the energy currents by running photonic and sonic healing frequencies that amplify and power up the original, undamaged Krystic blueprint throughout the planet. The anchoring of these Pillars ensures that Earth, as well as the entire Time Matrix, can receive ever higher levels of infusions of Source energy, and enable the whole Time Matrix to be shifted into healing the distortions, a cycle called the Healing Cycle of the Kryst.

The accumulation of structural damage that had been inflicted on the Earth template, including the templates of the higher expressions of Earth, (Earth's Soul Tara, and Earth's Oversoul or Monad Gaia) was such that without the Reuche Pillars these templates would not have been able to receive a high infusion of Source energy without overloading. The Reuche Pillars anchors from the highest frequency bands down through to the lowest frequency bands of Earth-Tara-Gaia moderating the levels of beneficial frequency that can be held by the damaged template structures to bring healing to the destruction encountered during the grid wars.

This damage had been forced on what is called the 'shield' of the planet, an energetic spinning disc of horizontal wave spectra which creates the scalar templates upon which the Hova bodies manifest (the Hova bodies hold our different Stations of Identity. There are five of these within the Time Matrix – Personality, Soul, Monad, or Oversoul, Avatar and Rishi or Solar – more on this later).

The Aurora Host

With the Reuche Pillars finally anchoring their energies this opened the way for the Mother essence, or Divine Mother energy of our Universe, to open up the larger creational fields and open Universal Core Gateways which allowed a **huge** amount of help from Light Beings from the neighbouring Universe to enter and come to our aid.

The immediate response and its magnitude are truly humbling as a flood of immense Light Beings answered the call and used the opening of these Gates to enter our Universe and begin the process of building out and installing new consciousness architectures, blueprints and various technologies to both repair the structural damage inflicted at many levels of our Time Matrix, and help release humanity from the alien technology used to enslave our mass consciousness.

This is called the Aurora Hosting project, sometime also referred to as the Failsafe Effort. It is truly an outpouring of love and support from other Light Beings and is ensuring that at every multidimensional, galactic and planetary level, the Source frequency energies can be sustained and permitted to flow freely, whilst undoing the damage inflicted by the Fallen races.

Incarnate on Earth at this time are lifeforms that hold a high template coding which will allow them to activate not just 12, but 24 – 48 strands of DNA potential, or up to 48 frequency bands of energy once they have moved beyond the Angelic Human Prototype form. These life-forms carry within their DNA template this high level of being able to hold 48 frequency bands under the right conditions. Many of these have been referred to as Starseeds.

These life-forms incarnating on Earth at this time have allowed Earth to receive the gift (from Source) of a *brand new shield* that is coded to the 24 – 48 DNA strands of these life-forms. These beings acted as the 'energy receivers' which allowed the new Higher Shield to be received and anchored into Earth's planetary template.

The Leap In Time

This produced a higher infusion of Source energy, which creates what is called a 'leap in time' and acts as a slight boost, rather like turning the dial slightly on a radio station to improve reception or pressing a little harder on the car accelerator to speed up. This infusion or 'leap in time' has enabled Earth to 'shift' slightly. This has been sufficient to pull it out of the danger zone of anything in alignment with the Fallen Races and their black hole system, so Earth is now free of this threat.

This leap in time has also allowed Earth and all life-forms and beings on it to return to the status of being 'Ascension Able', something that has been denied here for a long time due to the actions of the Fallen races. Earth is once more an Ascension Planet.

The Higher Shield that has been installed will enable more of the incoming Source energy to be held in Earth's fields and therefore ensure an ongoing process of healing to take place to damaged structures and templates. At least, that is true for all life-forms who <u>wish</u> to heal. Not all do, remember, and that is a choice allowed by Source. What these Fallen life-forms did NOT have the right to do was to block or impede those who did wish to follow the healing path of ascension, and this block has now been removed.

The life-forms of Earth can now begin to 'choose' a more balanced way of co-creating a new more harmonious reality field. They can choose to come together in communities and structures that are supportive of individual talents and aspirations as well as being pro-life, pro-human, pro-family and pro-individual empowerment. In the meantime those on the lower timeline, following the Fib-of-no-chi spiral will continue on in their warring paradigm of control and destruction.

The two will seem to exist side-by-side for a period, but it is of the highest importance that those who desire to heal and co-create something better 'wake up' and remember they are Source Embodied, they are a Divine Spark and need to quickly find an understanding of how their energetic structure works. This will help the final 'split' come sooner rather than later as the one 'reality' becomes more and more dissonant with the other.

Desire for healing alone will not bring about a rapid healing process, as each life-form has to learn to expand the energy quotient their template can hold once more, until it is up to full capacity. As humanity has been so degraded, there is a lot of ground to be made up, and it requires a deliberate effort to do this. We all have to learn to open up to and hold within ourselves ever greater levels of Source energy.

The thoughts, beliefs and behaviour a life-form or being carries plays a major role in the process of healing and being able to open up to greater levels of Source energy. It is essential that each individual remembers that this process begins *within* themselves, not through external agency, otherwise they will continue to allow themselves to be influenced by the thoughts of the old, lower energetic paradigm which those on the Krystic Spiral need to detach from.

Effectively, we need to 'update our software programme' to reflect the new reality and to ensure that our energetic frequency matches and builds on this.

It goes without saying that coming back to an understanding of how to regain control over one's personal energetic template structure is necessary at this time for the individual to understand the process of rebuilding their lightbody back into the full Krystal template or Diamond Sun DNA activation.

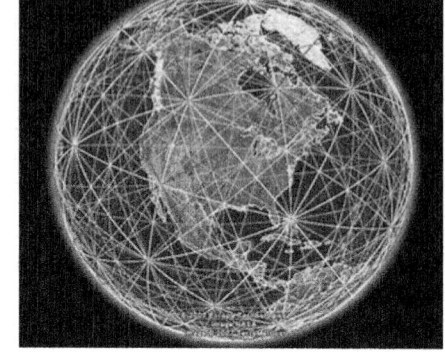

We shall look at this, and what we need to do later on.

Blocks to Ascension

The Fallen Angelics had in place many installed programmes and AI machinery all designed to block any ability to follow a true Ascension path. Some of these stretched through multi-dimensional levels and impacted whole areas of the Time Matrix, whilst others such as the unnatural NET fields were woven solely around the Earth.

The NET fields effectively form an energetic barrier around the Earth through which various frequencies and mind control programmes could be broadcast into the planetary grids, affecting all life-forms on Earth, and preventing 'escape' of the consciousness from these fields even after organic death.

It is good to know that these various fields and machinery are gradually beginning to dissolve and fall apart as the energy to sustain them, stolen from the planet's inhabitants, is beginning to go offline, and as life-forms begin to be able to move their frequency beyond their level of influence.

The distortions that have kept the life-forms of Earth from being able to complete the ascension process are held within the Emotional-Physical body level of anatomy as well as that part of planet Earth's anatomy. This is the level of energetic anatomy that a life-form must heal to allow them to ascend, which from our own personal point of view means clearing all of our negative beliefs, emotional traumas and behaviour patterns. All of this is held in the shadow body and is why doing our 'shadow work' is so important.

The 'Ascension Gate' opens 'within' a life-form that is able to accomplish the process of Ascension. It is not a gate that exists outside of yourself that you must go find and walk through. When a life-form or being is capable of completing the process of Ascension, this unfolds within them naturally and is as personal to their relationship with Source as the current death process is of removing our consciousness from the physical body form and leaving the 3-D reality field.

The process of accreting higher energy into one's personal template must occur by design and that which has been long taught on the Earth by the various Sacred Sciences is called 'Stair Step Creation' or the 'Stairway to Heaven'. It is effectively what it says – a step-by-step process of moving up the dimensional levels of the Time Matrix through gathering ever higher frequencies into the Lightbody, which begins to enable the transformation required that takes us back to our original activated Divine Template.

It is impossible for higher energy levels to be opened within the personal template unless the levels below that point are opened.

There are certain areas of knowledge that really enable us to actively work with this process of expanding consciousness and gathering ever higher frequencies into our Light bodies. Templar[6] mechanics, multidimensionality, our various Stations of Identity, our galactic families, Lightbody anatomy, and even our History,

---

[6] This refers to the energetic manifestation template or blueprint. The term is used for both the Planetary grids, shields and stargate systems and also can be used to refer to those with knowledge of the same and who work with it.

both universal and Earth-based, as this helps us understand why things occur as they currently do within the Earth reality fields, and what we are having to heal to get back on track. All this is the education we *should* have received as our birthright that has been denied to us by the Fallen Races.

What is Ascension?

Simply put, ascension is each individual activating their potential for god consciousness.

Sounds great doesn't it? But what does that really mean? There is obviously a lot more to the whole process than simply stating intent. I have come to realise over the many years of researching and seeking the answers to the simple question 'What is Ascension?' that this is not just a matter of certain mystical teachings, but there is a whole Sacred Science that lays out the process of Ascension.

It became apparent to me that the early Egyptian civilisation had a good handle on this, and practiced this art, but something happened to these teachings over the long course of this ancient civilisation and they became corrupted in some way, the pure teachings lost in superstition and 'black' magic.

Digging through the various wisdom streams I would catch glimpses of it again and again, but it was just that, a glimpse. Nothing seemed to have more to offer. Even the seemingly complete teachings of lore such are the Kabbalah felt incomplete and somehow 'off'.

In the teachings of the Avatar Jesus, and the early Gnostics, there were also something of this transcendent quality, but again they felt incomplete, vague and lacking in substance. It wasn't until I went 'galactic' as I called it, and started to open myself up to extradimensional levels of awareness that I started to find the information that made sense of what I had been looking for.

It came to me in all sorts of disjointed downloads and insights and nuggets of information which I have had to make sense of and align into their rightful order. Part of that process has simply been giving this area of investigation sufficient focus to sort through all the received information - there has been so much wonderful knowledge also incoming on fascinating topics such as Templar Mechanics, Galactic History, the Origins of Humanity and so on I became a little distracted. But the fast changing resonant frequencies and the clear shift in our reality and timeline have brought me back to this topic once more.

So let me share all I have come to understand.

We are all Sparks of the Divine, we have come from Source and with the organic ascension path, we seek to bring our consciousness back to wholeness and union with Source consciousness. It is a returning home, step-by-step, to where we originally came from.

Many teachings talk of the Out Breath of God and the In Breath of God. The out-breath is our journey from Source down into the matter dimensions of ever greater density. The in-breath is the return journey back to where we came from, taking with us the vast riches of experience our being has gained in the process.

Having come down into the lowest, most dense fields of matter of our Time Matrix or Universe, we have a long way to travel back home. But there is a clearly laid out map which has been available for us to follow – at least, that is, until fairly recent Earth history.

Earth is what is called an 'Ascension planet', one of many in the Universe. The straightforward and easy process of Ascension here is called 'Stairstep Ascension' or the 'Stairway to Heaven' and is facilitated via the Earth's Templar through the stargate portals.

Stellar Ascension Cycle (SAC)

Approximately every 26,000 years we enter into what is called a Stellar Activation Cycle. During this period the planetary universal stargates progressively align and open. This opens up portals to the next highest level, hence the term 'Stairstep Ascension'. It offers us the potential to move step-by-step from one level to the next.

As part of this SAC certain changes take place both within the planetary lightbody, as well as within our own. Effectively there is dissolution in the lower-dimensional layers of the consciousness fields.

Within our own lightbodies this is a dissolving of the chakra membranes between the three lower chakras, merging them together into one energy column as they move into the subharmonic levels of frequency of the next layer or density up.

Effectively, once our light body has accreted or gathered together all the subharmonic frequencies that make up a Harmonic Universe[7] or Density the particle layers begin to dissolve and those particles open into the lower subharmonics of the next Density level.

The same thing is happening at the level of the planetary lightbody and it is through these dynamics that both our consciousness and that of the planet progressively evolve step-by-step, moving up through the dimensional and density fields. Stellar activations are a natural and organic part of our evolution/ascension process which allows the vibrational pulsing of lower density layers to 'speed up' to match the pulsation rates of the next higher density levels. Effectively once the particle pulsation rates can begin to match those in the next highest

---

[7] Made up of three dimensional levels ie. Density 1 = Dimension 1, 2 and 3, Density 2 = Dimensions 4, 5, and 6

Harmonic Universe the energetic membranes or structures holding these in place dissolve to allow those particles to be drawn up or 'shifted' into the next level.

All of this takes place automatically and unconsciously for most of us and is a reflection of the vibrational level of our consciousness being in a state of preparedness for this window.

We are in the closing stages of a Stellar Activation Cycle at the time of writing this (2024), and whilst at the start of this Cycle (Year 2000) it was hoped that an unimpeded Stairstep process could take place, due to the immense damage sustained at various levels to Earth's Stargates and Templar structures it has not been viable. A different plan was immediately implemented, which I have talked about a little in the Introduction and I shall expand on later.

Lightbody Changes

Other changes take place in our lightbody depending upon the dimensional levels and stations of identity we are inhabiting, which we shall look at further on.

Our lightbody is the etheric energetic structure(s) from which our matter form emerges. The understanding of how sound and light energy become physical matter is basic metaphysical knowledge – and indeed the realm of quantum physics also explains this. It is also a basic teaching of Creation Mechanics.

As our consciousness begins to work its way back up through the dimensional layers, following the path of the Krystal Spiral back towards home, our matter body becomes less and less dense going from full physicality to semi-etheric, etheric and then full lightbody embodiment.

At the same time, changes are taking place in our lightbody to prepare us for the ability to transcend matter completely and be able to merge once more with the fields of first pre-matter, and then the great consciousness light fields at the highest frequencies of our Time Matrix, and the sound fields beyond that.

On this journey our lightbody heals the polarity split that has come in as a function of inhabiting the denser matter fields, and the distortions that have taken place here, and transforms itself into a vehicle for our consciousness to become part of these great fields once more, whilst still retaining the uniqueness of the Divine Spark that we represent.

Frequency

All of this requires our lightbody to expand to hold ever higher level of frequency and vibration as we move higher up the Time Matrix, without overloading and being damaged due to holding too much current without being properly prepared.

Those genuinely engaged in evolving their consciousness are actively seeking the means necessary to ensure this can happen, by undertaking practices that enable us to be continually stretching to reach the next layer of subharmonic frequencies....and the next....and the next. They are, to a large extent, summed up in the practices and teachings of the Law of One[8], Christos Teachings, which we will look at.

Trying to move frequencies through your lightbody (and physical body) before it is ready to hold those frequencies can lead to problems. Imagine pushing too much current through an electrical circuit – it blows a fuse! The same thing happens with us when too high a frequency is pushed through either an

---

[8] not to be confused with the Ra, Law of One Teachings, channelled by Ra, an alter ego for Marduk, an negative entity of Anunnaki origin.

unprepared lightbody or the physical body. You may have heard of 'spontaneous kundalini awakenings'. This refers to the spontaneous movement of energy from the root chakra to the crown in one instant and unexpected burst.

Preparation for this can lead to an altered state of consciousness, an opening of higher levels of awareness, but for those unprepared it can leave them appearing to be in the clutches of some kind of mental/emotional breakdown. Hopefully, after a period of healing they are able to re-stabilise, and begin to work gently with the expanding energies within, but many have their circuits blown and never fully recover. It can also cause long-term damage to the central nervous system.

Messing about with energy without fully understanding what it is you are trying to do, and the possible consequences, is not recommended.

Re-Activate Dormant DNA

Something I have not really mentioned so far is the part our DNA plays in this. The progenitors of the human race are the Oraphim from Density 3 of our Time Matrix, a race with a very advanced genetic makeup. They created the human race with a 12-strand DNA blueprint, which is called Diamond Sun DNA.

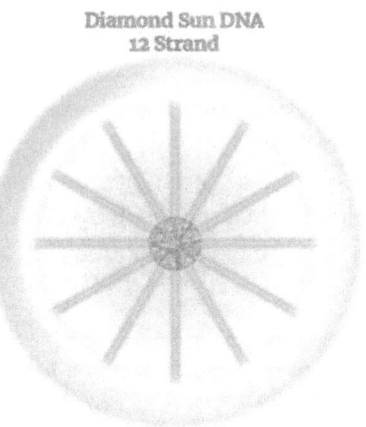

Diamond Sun DNA
12 Strand

Each strand of DNA relates to access to a dimensional level within the matter realms, and this alone tells us that when our blueprint is fully functioning and without distortions or mutations we are capable of running and holding, as a matter of course, 12th dimensional frequency currents.

Currently, the majority of humanity only has somewhere between 3 and 4 strands of DNA activated. That's a lot of de-activated potential!

Even our scientists, who tend to only see the world in terms of what is visible matter and the instruments they have to test it, admit that there is somewhere between 95 and 97% of our DNA which they called 'junk' ie. they can't discern any use for it.

One of the major tragedies for the human race has been not only how dense the vibration on earth has become (it used to be a lot lighter) but also how much of our DNA was deliberately mutated, de-activated and shut down.

And I do mean deliberately – this is not something we have knowingly done to ourselves. There have been outside forces that have planned and implemented this take-down very successfully.

There is quite a complex history behind this, which I shall write about at some point, but suffice it to say for now we here on Earth entered into a very Dark Age after the last Stellar Activation Cycle 26,000 years ago – a cycle where the opening of the stargates did not happen due to interference from Fallen races, who launched a plot at this time to ensure the *next* SAC did not happen either, and that by that time all of Earth's beings would be tightly under their control, so they could harvest the energy quanta of both the planet and her beings, as well as plunder her other resources, freely.

Gradually over the last 26,000 years great swathes of the energetic anatomy of our planet – the planetary Templar – has been taken over and infiltrated. Many organic grids have been invaded and machinery set up to run damaging reversal currents through them, artificial grids system overlays have implemented huge damage, stargate networks have been taken over, and much more besides.

Many of the advanced human bloodlines who were tasked with guardianship of the planetary Templar were targeted, hunted and massacred, until today only scattered remnants of these once potent bloodlines are left.

All of this has led to not only the drop in frequency but immense damage to the planetary consciousness networks, to which we are so closely aligned. Inevitably the damage has been felt within our own energetic anatomy.

The most devastating blow came around 5,500 years ago when, due to an event called the Sumerian/Babylonian Invasion and Massacre, the 4th Stargate Solar network was captured.

As a result, much of our DNA was unplugged through the insertion of alien machinery into the energy grids which resulted in not just the DNA de-activation and consequent inability to hold higher frequencies and access many of our inherent abilities, but also in a racial mind wipe as we were cut off from accessing the levels of our DNA which held our racial history and origins, knowledge of our DNA language, and our higher purpose.

At the physical level major glandular imbalances and disease occurred as we became unable to heal ourselves and early death – threescore years and ten – became our reality, where beforehand much longer lifespans had been our legacy.

It was a devastating blow. The enslavement of humanity was well under way and within a few generations very few retained any memory of what had happened as alterative narratives were fed to the survivors.

Those narratives have changed over the ages according to who is in control of the agenda (there are various factions within the Fallen races, all vying for dominance) and how they want to manipulate us.

Much of humanity is still passive and unconscious today – cut off, through de-activated DNA, from accessing both race and soul memories, as well as communicating with their higher stations of identity[9], unable to access higher sensory perception, unaware of our multidimensionality and galactic families.

Rebuilding, repairing and re-activating each strand of DNA is part of the work that has to be done by any being here on Earth on the Ascension path, gradually bringing our template back to a state of full activation and wholeness.

Again, I think it helps to understand what we are trying to do, but it is our *actions*, the way we behave, the thoughts and beliefs we hold, the emotional field we build that all hold a vibrational frequency and contribute to the healing and re-activation of our energetic anatomy, including our etheric DNA.

We can sit down and set a clear and powerful intent for our DNA to be healed, but it is our actions (service to Other versus service to Self), thoughts, beliefs and energetic frequency field we build that will bring that healing and re-activation.

And that is a choice we all individually have to make – to commit to the Ascension path, to commit to taking back mastery of our thoughts and emotions, to unplugging our energy fields from the negativity being broadcast into our homes and consciousness through television, phones, computers, wi-fi and 'smart' networks, mind control AI programmes and much else besides.

To be on the Ascension path is to work to become a sovereign being, whose consciousness is under your own individual control, not influenced or directed by **any** outside forces, a being who

---

[9] There are 5 Stations of Identity we all hold within the Time Matrix and another 3 held within the Energy Matrix. Each of the 5 domains corresponds to a Density level – Personality, Soul, Monad, Avatar and Rishi or Solar Matrix.

rejects any attempts to control, enslave dominate or in any way constrict the choices you have and how you choose to live your life.

In doing so you build a field of frequency around yourself that not only heals, little-by-little, each strand of DNA, but opens up to you layer-by-layer the multidimensional fields of this Time Matrix which are your legacy, and returns you to the wholeness of who you REALLY are – a Christos Human being, one of the galactic races who hold the spark of the Divine within, who has the ability, when the full body template is activated, to travel the many levels and layers of not only this Time Matrix, but beyond.

THIS is who you truly are, and what you have forgotten.

Multidimensionality Basics

This is worthy of a book in itself for, if we are going to stand any chance of getting our heads around the ascension process and how to engage in it, we need a basic understanding of multi-dimensionality, what we mean by this term and what it looks like and how we engage with it.

The following is a brief outline which will hopefully be enough to give you the basics concepts to have a simple understanding of the energetic structure of our Universe.

We live in a 15-dimensional Time Matrix or Universe, of which there are countless others in the vastness of Creation. Our Time Matrix is structured around a vast morphogenetic field which holds our entire multidimensional universe within in.

The 15 dimensions are grouped into 5 different Densities or Harmonic Universes, or you may sometimes hear them referred to as Triads.

>Harmonic Universe or Density 1 Dimensions 1, 2 and 3
>Harmonic Universe or Density 2 Dimensions 4, 5 and 6
>Harmonic Universe or Density 3 Dimensions 7, 8 and 9
>Harmonic Universe or Density 4 Dimensions 10, 11 and 12
>Harmonic Universe or Density 5 Dimensions 13, 14 and 15

Each dimension reflects a different frequency, with the highest frequencies being at the top of the Time Matrix (dimensions 13, 14, 15), and the lowest at the bottom (dimensions 1, 2, 3).

Each Harmonic Universe or density describes different levels of consciousness and being. Humanity has been in one of the lowest, the 3rd dimensional field of Density or Harmonic Universe (HU) 1, and with this Ascension cycle is looking to shift into the next Density up (HU2 dimensions 4, 5,6).

15 Dimensional Time Matrix

Primary Sound Fields of Source Energy/Consciousness Matrix

HU	Dimension	Matrix Level	Description
HU 5	D.15 D.14 D.13	Solar Rishi/ Solar Dragon Matrix Home of the Trifold Flame Blue/Gold/Violet	3 Primary rays of sound and light No matter, no time Home of Eieyani Council or Founder Races
HU4	D.12 D.11 D.10	Avatar Level Matrix	Entry point into densification of matter Non-physical pre-matter template Hydroplasmic Christos liquid light field Solar Logos & Solar Dragon fields
HU3	D.9 D.8 D.7	Oversoul (monadic) level Matrix	Etheric Home of Planetary Logos or Mind (D7), Galactic Core (D8), Causal Body (D9) HU 3 home of 7D planet Gaia
HU2	D.6 D.5 D.4	Soul level Matrix	Semi-Etheric Home of Astral and Emotional Body (D4), Archetypal Body (D5), Celestial Body (D6) HU 2 home of 5D planet Tara
HU1	D.3 D.2 D.1	Personality level Matrix	Full physicality Home of Subconscious Intelligence (D1), Instinctual Intelligence (D2) and Conscious Mind Intelligence (D3) HU 1 home of 3D planet Earth

HU = Harmonic Universe or density
www.sairasalmon.com   ©S Salmon 2024/11

The illustration on the previous page is a linear view of the Time Matrix, and it can help to get the multidimensionality concept fixed in your head to think of it this way initially as linear concepts come more easily to us in 3D.

But ultimately we have to come to understand this as a *nested* multi-layered universe, rather like a set of Russian dolls, with the lowest dimensions the ones in the centre, surrounded by ever greater and larger dimensions as we expand up the frequency scale.

You can see from the illustration that each of the Densities or Harmonic Universes has a Matrix or what is called a Station of Identity assigned to it.

We are going to look at what this means in more detail further on, but each level refers to an aspect of our light body. When we are whole, working from a fully healed and working 12-strand DNA template, we inhabit a huge consciousness which can span and travel easily through all 12 matter and pre-matter levels of the Time Matrix, before merging into the sound and light fields.

Here in Density 1, within the Personality Matrix we should be in contact with the other layers of Self. This is one of the things the Fallen races have taken from us by isolating Earth and shutting down our DNA for thousands of years. This is just beginning to open back up to us, and those of us aware of these other levels of Self are making contact once more – a joyful reunion!

But most are totally unaware of these other levels of Self, and therefore it doesn't even occur to them to re-establish their connection.

I have talked about energy moving in an expanding upward spiral, and each level or 'station' on this spiral contains a more complete part of Self that we merge back into as we move back through the densities – our Personality Self merges into our Soul Self, merges into our Oversoul and then our Avatar and so on. At each level our physical body goes through changes, from a carbon-base to eventually a fully crystalline light being.

Subharmonics

Within each dimensional band of frequency there are what are called subharmonics. Every band has 12 subharmonics that make up the full dimensional frequency band. One by one we accrete these subharmonic frequencies into our light body, until we have 'gathered in' all the harmonics of that frequency band, and we start on the next.

As each dimension has 12 subharmonics, and there are three dimensions in a density band or Harmonic Universe 3 x 12 = 36 subharmonics in each density that we have to attune and expand into and merge into our lightbody as we move through the layers.

Dimensions, Frequencies, Timelines

These words are used more or less interchangeably. Each dimension exposes us to a different frequency, and to a different reality or timeline – it is like the difference between the view of a ground-based bird and an eagle. The landscape is the same, but it is viewed from a very different perspective and expanded horizon.

At each different level there is a change in the focus of our consciousness as the frequency increases. The shift from one density or Harmonic Universe to the next understandably brings about a greater shift of focus, as we move from a more concentrated matrix level of our being to a more expanded level. Consciousness is energy, and as the energy shifts and changes so does our consciousness.

As we move the focus of our consciousness into the next frequency or timeline – what is often referred to as a *future* Timeline – then we enter a different plane of existence. Usually the exposure to this is gradual, so the shift can be very subtle, and if we are not aware of what we are undergoing, it can be missed, but at this moment in time, with a major shift and release under way, I would suggest that most of us are aware to some level or other of how great a change is taking place in our perception of reality.

The move into a higher level of frequency will also be opening up the potential, should you choose to develop it, to access into various innate abilities that were shut down or denied to us under the frequency NETs and mind control mechanisms that characterized the imposed control conditions of the Fallen races in 3D.

What might this mean for you? Almost certainly you will become aware of your 'Soul' Self, or Higher Self, as it is often referred to. Your intuition will definitely be much sharper and more apparent – although, of course, you still have to be prepared to listen and act on it, not ignore it!

Many will find that latent psi senses begin to open up, or that the ability to begin to tap into the up until now hidden history of our race on earth expands, as well as becoming more aware of our galactic families and histories. Your inner knowing or 'Gnosis' may begin to refine into a strong and clear current you can follow, and you will definitely be able to strengthen both your connection to your 'guides' or soul family, as well as that to Source.

Physically you should feel lighter, as many of the emotional traumas and mental straight-jackets we found ourselves in will have had to be shed to get to where we are going.

Naturally, your ability to access all of this requires you to be both aware of what is happening and willing to have an open enough mind to explore the expanding levels of consciousness and what they bring without shutting anything down through fear or resistance to change.

Of course, there are plenty who will find themselves in a state of fear and resistance as they feel 'out of sorts' with the resonant energies that make up the backdrop of their lives. If you are still fully brain-washed by the Fallen race agenda, and are unwilling, unprepared or even unaware that you need to update your programme to the new realities, the more dissonant your mental/emotional state becomes to the prevailing background energies the more uncomfortable and unbalanced you will feel.

All those who are resonant with the prevailing energies will have done the hard work of clearing emotional blockages and traumas, of working through outdated beliefs and thought forms, and of beginning to see through the many control structures, agendas and false narratives that kept humanity passive and enslaved throughout the Dark Aeon we are emerging from.

It becomes a free will choice whether those who are struggling decide to do the work and shed the burdens to match the frequency or not. Some, although their Higher Self may be willing, may find it all but impossible due to sustained DNA damage or traumas to shed what is holding them back, and it is likely these will put down this physical body – the 3D template that will not transmute – and be re-born into a 5D template body in order to move forward.

And, of course, there are those who do NOT want the status quo to change, who do NOT want to act more kindly and compassionately towards their fellow man, who do NOT want to make any kind of evolutionary advance. And that is fine. Their resonant frequency will remain low, part of the lower fields and they will stay on the lower timeline, and follow that path wherever it leads as the two timelines begin to separate more and more over the next few years.

Multidimensional Earth

Just as we have different stations of identity within each Harmonic Universe, so does Earth.

Here in Density 1 we know our planet and its dimensional consciousness and timelines as Earth. Here we have the histories – hidden and otherwise – that relate to humanity's seedings on this planet over the span of linear time we have inhabited here in this density.

In Harmonic Universe or Density 2, the next higher level of our planet's consciousness is called Tara, and we talk of the Taran histories and fall of these times. This is Earth's Soul body.

In Harmonic Universe or Density 3, the higher dimensional iteration of Earth at 7D is called Gaia, and once again has its own history of invasion, wars and catastrophes which we might think of as being in our past, although Gaia is *future* 5D or ascended Tara. Gaia is Earth's Monad body.

This is where beginning to get your head around a basic understanding of the nature of time becomes necessary otherwise you will struggle to make sense of this. At one level Tara is *future* Earth, as that is the higher consciousness level of Earth we are moving into. But also, in a linear interpretation of time – and remember time is a construct we use in the lower matter fields to make sense of our reality – Tara tells us stories of our *past*.

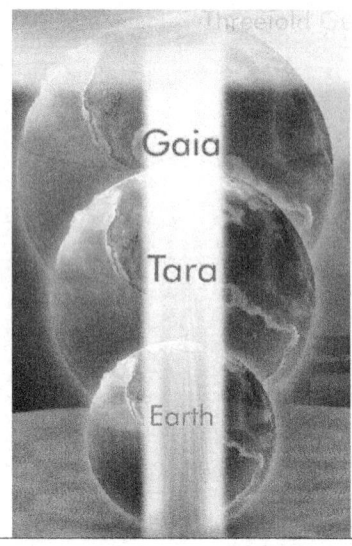

For example, the human race, called the Turaneusiam, were originally seeded on 5D Tara, and lived there for many millions of years before the cataclysm that struck Tara, causing some of her morphogenetic fields to fall into the deeper densities of Harmonic Universe 1, along with many fragmented and lost souls.

The seeding of humanity on 3D Earth, and the long history that has played out here happened very much as a function of this catastrophe, and part of every being's purpose here has been to help rescue the lost and fragmented souls from the Taran histories, as well as the Gaian.

Earth herself has been 'rescuing' the lost morphogenetic fields of Tara, so as she merges once more with her 5D Self she can heal this wounding.

And all of this is taking place in the NOW.

Because, in reality there is no past or future, there is only the NOW.

Remember what I said about the dimensional fields not really being a dimensional ladder, but a *nested* group of fields? Within each Harmonic Universe the histories are all playing out now – the catastrophic invasion of Gaia and its consequences, ditto the Fall of Tara, and then the way these repeating histories

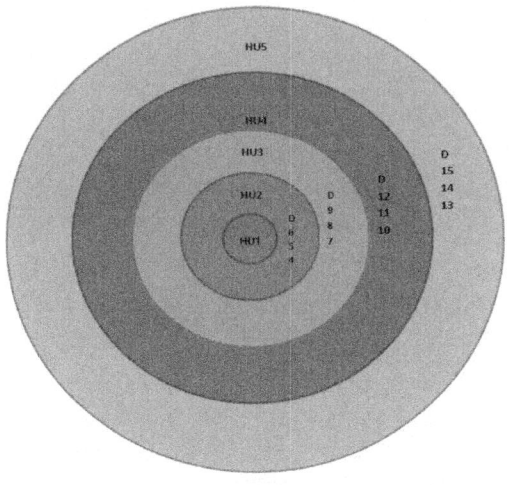

15-Dimensional Universe, 5 Nested Harmonic Universes

have shown up on the Earth plane – the destruction of Lemuria, the Fall of Atlantis and so on.

I know this can be quite hard to get your head around – and I am far from being an expert on this, it makes my brain hurt too! – but this is the only way it makes sense to me when I look at all of our different dimensional histories, trying to understand the seeming anomalies from a linear perspective.

In the next layer over from the one we reside in, next door if you like, but a next door we are largely unaware of and cannot see, and next door to that also and so on, all of this is playing out.

It also helps to make sense of time travel. There are some galactic races who are Time Portal Mechanics experts and can drop in and out of different points on the various timelines. The ET race the Greys, who are one of the Fallen races here on Earth, are said to be able to do this by opening 'wormholes' between the layers, although I am sure there must be less destructive ways of achieving this as well.

Multidimensional DNA

I have already mentioned that our DNA holds a 12-strand potential when it is fully activated and healed, but I want to dive just a little bit deeper into what this really means.

As I said, each strand of DNA relates to access to a dimensional level within the matter realms. As a result every fully activated and functional strand of DNA means that the individual consciousness can access that level of dimensionality.

DNA is not simply chemical molecules in your body. I have heard it described as a multidimensional piece of Divinity, which is not an exaggeration. Our DNA reflects the instruction sets and blueprints of the many-layered complex structures and architectures that go to make up creation.

It acts as both a transmitter and receiver drawing in and transmitting energy from and into the energy fields around us. Unless we are fully sovereign in our thoughts, beliefs, emotional mastery etc we can be programmed from this field.

It connects us into the holographic matrices which make up our universal galactic layers as well as connecting us into the planetary grid network through its electromagnetic qualities. It is said that DNA holds all the information we will ever need in order to build and maintain the human body in health.

This is also true at the lightbody level, with which our DNA connects. It is designed to integrate the polarities that are so prevalent around us, and enables us to access the huge information fields of light and sound (consciousness) that surround us, no matter which dimensional level we are at.

If our 12-strand DNA is working as it should, this template enables every human to embody all 12 dimensions of consciousness, as well as easily access interdimensional travel, and maintain a form which is not subject to deterioration ie. immortal, as well as many other wonders besides.

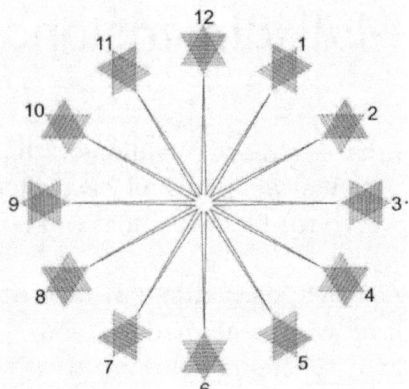

This is your heritage. This is what the whole process of ascension or evolution is helping you reclaim.

Due to the immense damage and mutation which has been sustained, much of it deliberate, some of it a byproduct of what we have been exposed to, a majority of human life-forms on the planet today have been reduced to 3 – 4 functioning strands, and are actively working to repair and activate the 5th strand. There are those who have achieved this and also have an activated 6th strand[10], and there are a few, a very few who have progressed beyond this.

Our spiritual evolution does not happen without DNA activation, it is part and parcel of the journey we are on.

At Dimension 1 – 3, strands 1 – 3 we incarnate in a physical body and identify with this physical body. As we move into the next level we become more aware of the auric/energy body and this begins to expand and accrete light from dimensions 4, 5 and 6.

Once strand 6 is activated we are fully embodied as a Soul

---

[10] See chapter The Role of Starseeds, Indigos and Lightworkers

identity. A Soul in this state is living fully aligned with their mission and authentic soul expression, and exercises their free will solely in service to Source or Divine will.

As we start into the next level of embodiment and activation we begin to activate the Oversoul identity, also called the Monad. Finally we come to dimensions 10, 11 and 12 with the embodiment of the Christos Avatar identity where, once the 12th strand is fully activated we become a living Avatar, we can manifest and de-manifest our physical vessel at will, and have full control of biological transmutation.

Effectively as we move through the stages our physical matter body changes from being fully carbon-based to silica-based, then fully etheric before becoming a vessel of liquid light plasma.

There is more, a lot more, to share around understanding this subject but I will write in much more depth about this in my upcoming book *Building the Light Body*, which will go in depth into our Lightbody anatomy.

Let us finish this topic with some channeled information from the Pleiadians, shared by Barbara Marciniak in her 1995 book *The Pleiadian Agenda.* There they answer the question so many people have about 12-strand DNA – we only physically see 2 strands, so where are the missing 10 strands?

The missing 10 strands aren't physical, they are etheric. They were 'unplugged' according to the Pleiadians 300,000 years ago to the 2 strands we are familiar with[11] . The remaining 10 light-encoded filaments were disconnected and our goal now is to

---

[11] Scientists agree that our DNA shown signs of outside interference, but they put a time of 200 – 250,000 years ago on this, although this is purely at the physical level of course. See Gregg Braden *The Science of Self-Empowerment*

reconnect these disabled strands.

They tell us that the 'Original Planners' called on the 'Family of Light' to incarnate into the Earth system in human bodies in order to help with the reactivation and healing back to the original blueprint. [12]

They also said 'The task you have before you is to consciously command, intend, and will the evolvement of your DNA,' and, 'The light-encoded filaments carry the language of light geometry, which carries the stories of who you are.'

This, they finished by saying, is the time in which humanity changes and literally becomes multidimensional beings.

Clearly, exciting times ahead!

---

[12] See chapter The Role of Starseeds, Indigos and Lightworkers

Multidimensional Self or Stations of Identity

I have mentioned earlier what are called Stations of Identity also referred to as the Hova bodies.

Looking at the diagram of the structure of the universe we can see what they are:

> HU1 – Personality/Ego Matrix
> HU2 – Soul Matrix
> HU3 – Oversoul/Monad Matrix
> HU4 – Avatar Matrix
> HU5 – Rishi Matrix

But what does this mean?

Each refers to a level of consciousness intelligence, or a layer of consciousness body.

Personality Matrix

At the 3D level we have only a limited perception of the true nature of reality and the world around us, with our perception being largely limited to the physical world of the 5 senses.

The Personality Matrix projects 3D consciousness into the body through the first 3 chakras – the 1st Chakra of the Unconscious Mind, the 2nd Chakra of the Instinctual Mind and the 3rd Chakra of the Conscious or Ego Mind.

Someone who functions solely from the Personality Matrix, is much more likely to be more developed at the mental than the emotional level, and will dismiss all multidimensional and Higher

Sense perception experiences of those further advanced as nonsense. The intellect rules!

Soul Matrix

The Soul Matrix is often referred to as the first level of awakening, and holds the principles of creative imagination, receptivity and feeling perception. This matrix also acts as the repository of the accumulated memories of the individual consciousness, which are recorded into the cellular matrix of this body.

It works through the 'higher' chakras. At the 4th chakra the Heart centre opens and emotional intelligence develops. This is often seen as being the first level of divinity and heart intelligence. The 5th chakra is also called the Archetypal body and sets the patterns for our etheric body, and here Ego will begin to fully give way to Higher will.

The 6th chakra is that of Inner Vision and Higher Sense perception and higher vision begin to open up more fully. The Indigo races incarnate on Earth with this DNA strand activated.

Oversoul or Monad Matrix

The Oversoul or Monad refers to the 7D-8D-9D layers of the lightbody and it is here we begin to not only realise the actuality of the holographic architectures of our reality, but also to synthesize the Planetary Logos or brain into embodiment. Where once might see the Soul Matrix as being the Heart complex, the Monad is the Brain complex, and the Heart-Brain begin their merge.

This Higher Mind complex acts as the Observer, able to maintain a neutral stance and make decisions from this higher evolutionary space.

At the 7th chakra the Crown activates and the 7 chakra column within the physical body become a unified column of energy, opening us into full awareness of our unity with the planetary consciousness and her grids. This could be called the Guardian level where this realization of our guardian role of the planet is fully understood.

At the 8th chakra level Galactic awareness begins to open up along with the Higher Heart energies which activates a configuration within the light body called the Living Crystal Lotus Heart or Crystal Rose Heart.

The 9th chakra is also called the Atomic Doorway, or Mouth of God. We expand into a sense of connection with all things, and easily maintain ourselves in this enlarged field.

At the monadic level the negative Ego is no more and personal will takes a back seat over Divine Will. We begin to move into our Divine Purpose and align with this. Until we have embodied this aspect of our spiritual intelligence we are unable to manifest fully this Divine Purpose. When we have achieved this we no longer need to keep seeking our purpose, it becomes fully apparent.

Avatar Matrix

Also called the Christos Avatar matrix, once this is fully embodied it represents the highest expression of consciousness of the original Divine Human templating. It is here we embody the Christ Consciousness currents, and truly start our merge fully into the unity fields.

The three levels of frequency of the Christos fields are the $10D/10^{th}$ chakra of Krystic or Christ mind, the $11D/11^{th}$ chakra of Buddhic mind and the $12D/12^{th}$ chakra of Solar Logos or full unity consciousness.

Once we have fully embodied this our body is fully crystalline as a hydroplasmic liquid light blueprint, and we have access to universal consciousness and all cellular memory records. We naturally fully commit to service to the Law of One.

Ascension Stages

As I have described previously, Ascension is a shift in energetic frequency, from a lower frequency, whether that be a density, a dimension or a subharmonic, to a higher one. At the same time we are in a process of slowly embodying the many layers of light that make up our spiritual body into matter, and anchoring them in at each level.

This whole process catalyzes our energetic template, according to the Individual instruction sets it has (and every being's instructions sets are unique to their personal journey) to transmute and transform certain patterns and programmes at each level of our Self into those appropriate for the next.

Thus we exchange a 3D templating for a 5D templating, and then a 5D for a 7D/8D and so on.

This will initiate a clearing at each level that may be felt mentally, emotionally and even physically as what are called Ascension symptoms. The Dark Night of the Soul is one phase of spiritual crisis 'clearing' which many are familiar with. This is the start of releasing Negative Ego from our fields, and is an essential part of the 'die-off' or purging of emotions/beliefs to drop density. Remember, both our physical body is changing as we move to ever higher frequencies as well as our light body, and we need to 'lighten our load' to achieve these frequencies.

So there is a need to purge the Negative Ego as well as release the Pain Body, and become a self-sustained being drawing our life force from the Source fields, and not other beings.

There are three major steps or stages to this process: Initiation – Absorption – Integration. So let's look further at each in turn.

Initiation

The first stage of this process is Spiritual Initiation. This is not necessarily a one-off process, as it happens every time there is an influx of kundalini Spirit or Higher Consciousness into the body. In some respects it could be likened to the process of 'breakdown to break through'. After each initiation the physical body has to transmute density so what does this mean in reality?

There has to be a 'dying' to conventional, conditioned structures at the levels of belief, and toxic emotions and traumas are often revisited in order to be released. Hanging on to perceived 'wounds' and victim consciousness is a real brake on allowing the process to move freely through as it should. Physically this will also be felt as the body goes through a detoxification of physical impurities and imbalances. We shall look at some of these ascension symptoms shortly, but it can be difficult and scary if you do not understand what is happening.

For some people this is experienced as a huge and spontaneous kundalini movement up the spine, dumping them into spiritual crisis almost immediately as their body and psyche struggles to understand and integrate what is happening. For those who have no understanding of what is happening, nor an spiritual mentor to help, it is highly likely they will end up on strong drugs and labelled as having 'mental problems' at this time, which only makes it more difficult for them to win through. Our Society lacks insight and understanding about what is really required.

Most of us, fortunately, experience the process as a slower, more step-by-step opening up of the kundalini energies, making it easier to handle – although it is not a cake-walk by any means. Our environment in deep density, and the energy fields that surround us, can be likened to a rather unhealthy swamp and we need to clear down to be as near to a 'pure mountain stream' as we can get.

So the first ascension stage is Initiation, during which incoming spiritual energies will activate our DNA, and effect a process of clearing and transmutation from our physical body through to all layers of our energy body. It can be likened to the process of initiating an update of both our computer hardware (physical body) and the software that it runs.

The body will begin to accrete sub-harmonic by sub-harmonic the new electromagnetic light codes, which instruct and prepare the neurological structures and neural networks to open the way for ever higher frequencies to be received. With any luck, the body/psyche acclimates to this slowly and gradually without major trauma.

Absorption

The next stage of Ascension is that of absorption. Once the body is receiving the new electromagnetic frequencies, those frequencies need to be absorbed into the energetic/spiritual bodies and aura. At the same time light accretion takes place.

Once again this process is unique to each individual as it will trigger the clearing process already mentioned to ensure these new, higher frequencies can anchor in. Various things may surface within the psyche – karmic lessons perhaps, unresolved conflicts and traumas, issues where our sovereignty is weak, past life woundings or lessons, present time conflict. All will be seeking resolution and release.

As the new frequencies encounter energy blockages, these will have to be cleared, either through spiritual work or with the help of a skilled energy therapist. Miasms, False White Light and Dead Energy are all likely to be encountered and require to be purged to make progress.

As this spiritual progress is achieved it will clear the way for greater connection to ever-expanding levels of consciousness and our higher intelligence and the higher sense perception of our spiritual identity. Depending upon the individual this will be experienced in various ways, as hidden gifts and tools embedded in each individual's blueprint are accessed.

As more and more light accretes and becomes firmly anchored into the body, the more visible we make ourselves to those who do not wish us well – Fallen races, particularly those inhabiting the lower fourth dimensional levels, can identify more easily the beacons of light we are becoming and attempt to attack, derail or otherwise control the individual. We have to ensure strong shielding, strong psychic hygiene and stand firm in our sovereignty and self-mastery to withstand the attacks.

The attempts to 'take down' those who are successfully ascending will not stop, but if we maintain good discipline they will become ever less effective.

Integration

The final stage is integration, and it is here that, once the maximum frequency absorption has been achieved, the Chakras and DNA activate to firmly integrate these new frequencies and light codes into the physical body and initiate the changes that will take place at this level. New neural networks will be formed, telepathic abilities are likely to open up ever further and a greater sense of multidimensionality, new perceptions and energy sensitivity will be felt.

If the individual is totally unprepared for these changes it can trigger a spiritual crisis as it can be very disorientating with the shifting perception of 'reality'.

Ascension Symptoms

As you can infer from all of the above, there are likely to be many signs and symptoms as the ascension process unfolds. It can feel very debilitating at times as your body template and physical structure are 're-wired' and transmuted to suit the new reality that one is moving into.

Emotional, mental, physical and even spiritual-energetic levels of our being can feel at times like they are under assault. I have mentioned the Dark Night of the Soul which can be a very painful and overwhelming experience, but clearing old traumas, family wounds, finding many of our 'beliefs' are wrong, that reality is not what we thought it to be and so on can all cause a level of suffering and disorientation.

It can also be very hard on the physical body. Here are just a few of the more common symptoms that can be experienced:

Debilitating fatigue	Disorientation/vertigo
Disturbed sleep	Body and muscle aches
Headaches/pressure in head	Irritability
Flu-like symptoms	Skin rashes
Waves of heat	Nerve tingling/numbness
Memory loss/forgetfulness	Vision problems
Loss of focus/concentration	Joint pains

In addition there may be a few days of purging in some form – diarrhea or nosebleeds maybe. Anxiety attacks may come and go even if you are not prone to them, or you may begin to see multidimensional energies or beings or even light codes and colours, have psychic experiences, become clumsier for a while or there may be very uncomfortable bursts of energy or heat that seems to move through the body in a wave. It is a unique experience for each of us.

Remember, much higher levels of light are entering our body fields and we are literally being recalibrated. A lot of this may take place at night resulting in poor sleep quality and feeling tired in the morning.

It goes without saying really that you need to be gentle with yourself. If you have to rest, do so. Do not push yourself to exhaustion. Support your body with drinking plenty of water, using herbs and good nutrition to support any body symptoms you may have and generally working to open and expand your consciousness fields to embrace the process that is unfolding, rather than being in resistance.

Having a clear understanding of the context of what is occurring can make a huge difference to the way in which Ascension and its processes and symptoms are handled. Those who are unaware are likely to resist many of the changes taking place, blocking or preventing the process unfolding, as well as misidentifying much of what is happening as worrying medical symptoms.

Being free of fear and confusion moving through this process enables it to unfold more speedily and integrate more rapidly.

The Different Paths Back to Source

As already mentioned, we live in a Time Matrix or Universe where the main process of Ascension is through what is called Stair Step Ascension or the Stairway to Heaven.

It effectively describes an Ascension process that has us move through the multidimensional frequencies and sub-harmonics literally one-by-one, accreting each frequency and sub-harmonic frequency into our lightbody before moving onto the next.

When we have accreted all the various frequencies in one Density or Harmonic Universe, we then make the shift to the next Density and begin to work from the lowest to the highest frequency levels of the 3 dimensions and 36 sub-harmonics of that one and so on.

Once we have moved through the 9 fields of matter, we then progress into the 3 fields of pre-matter, before entering the light fields and moving onto the sound fields beyond that, should that be what we choose. It is a steady, orderly, well-laid out path of evolution along the path of the Krystal Spiral back into the Source fields.

As we progress on this path we move from biological carbon form, through silicate to crystalline etheric form and from there to more complex structures of pure consciousness identity.

In order to successfully go through this process we have to address and heal many issues, not least of which is clearing trauma, dis-ease, fear, ego-identity, shadow self, alien AI implants, in order to reclaim our sovereign consciousness. We also have to claim back any fragments of consciousness, body parts, or other aspects of Self that may have been lost, stolen, hijacked or otherwise taken from us through the many wars, catastrophes, suffering, ordeals, torture and mishaps that may have occurred to aspects of Self during the long aeons our consciousness has been within this Time Matrix.

Phew! Sounds like quite a task doesn't it? Never forget though that you are an immortal Soul and have been working on this process of coming back to wholeness for many human lifetimes. Little-by-little it is a process of coming back into unity with not just the true authentic expression of who you are, but also of coming back into unity with all Life, as we are all part of the same whole.

For this reason, you may also sometimes hear this path referred to as the Stardust Return Wholeness path.

This is not the only path back to Source, which is just as well, as Stairstep Ascension requires that we can access the planetary universal stargates, as they come into alignment with the galactic, multidimensional stargate networks during a Stellar Activation Cycle.

This has been unable to happen this time, as I mentioned earlier, due to the immense damage that has been sustained to the planetary Templar and stargate networks. If we were left to our own devices here on planet Earth it would have been game over, in favour of the Fallen races, but we are far from on our own.

Many, many galactic races from many levels of our Time Matrix have never abandoned us even during our darkest hours. Whilst there was a period where the Fallen races had managed to isolate Earth from what they saw as 'interference' from beyond – or what we would have called rescue missions – that has not been the case for some years now, and many races have not only sent volunteers here into this deep density to incarnate into a human body[13] in order to give boots-on-the-ground help and assistance to negate and help correct much of the damage inflicted by the Fallen Races, but there are vast legions of galactic, multi-dimensional and extra-dimensional beings who have answered the call and come to the assistance of not just our planet, but this Time Matrix.

Earth, you see, is not the only place that the Fallen races have attempted to trash and divert into fallen consciousness. Areas of the Time Matrix have sustained vast damage too, and the decision was taken that the time for this to end is now.

The Fallen races imposed their will on other races, many of whom are unconscious to a large degree of what is being inflicted on them, such as here on Earth, but also many of whom are conscious but deeply enslaved. In a Free Will universe this is no longer acceptable. More than sufficient time has been given for Fallen races to correct their mistakes or, as we might say in somewhat old-fashioned language today, to repent!

Before the damage goes beyond being able to heal, legions of Christos beings are here to ensure it goes no further and reverse the process. Every time I connect into any aspect of those who are 'out there' fighting on our behalf a spiritual war for human consciousness I am moved and humbled beyond measure by the unconditionality of the response from other Christos beings, the love they have for us and for all Life, and their determination to correct the terrible imbalances which have occurred here.

So we are far from alone, the help we have is overwhelming, and little-by-little they have been doing their best to correct some of the worst atrocities committed to the planetary Templar.

---

[13] See chapter the Role of Starseeds, Indigos and Lightworkers

Unfortunately the damage to the stargates, to permit Stairstep Ascension at this time, was so extensive as to not be able to be repaired before the Stellar Ascension Cycle ended. But all is not lost for the many of us desperate to move on from this 3D prison we have been trapped within for millennia.

A new plan to ensure all who want to evolve can do so was implemented. You may hear this referred to Ascension Plan B, or the Mother Arc and Aurora Hubs.

So what does Ascension Plan B entail? I envisage it as a subtle side-step to bypass the damaged stargate network. Instead a whole network of gates which have not been operative on the planet for a long time, the Mother Arc gates, which connect into the Divine Mother energy of the 13th dimensional field have been re-opened and powered up little-by-little.

Each win, as the alien intruders were ousted from the primary consciousness grids of the Earth, as their dark nests and entities and abominations have been cleared out, has opened the way for the return of the Divine Mother energies to this planet, which had been denied access to not only this planet but the Time Matrix for aeons[14].

Many have worked in various ways and various levels to ensure the Return of the Divine Feminine to this system, and to clear out the poisonous influence of the Dark Mother energies of the alien invasion.

As a result of this success it has allowed the extra-dimensional Aurora races to build out what are called Aurora Hubs or Platforms. These effectively provide safe space which, putting it

---

[14] The 12th Universal Stargate on the 12th dimensional planet Aramatena was deliberately blown up, so nothing could either enter or leave.

very simplistically, allow us to 'step over' the various Frequency Fences and NETs[15] that are operated by the Fallen races to ensure nothing 'escapes' Harmonic Universe or Density 1 – including us!

These Aurora platforms guide the ascending energies of our planet and its life-forms through Arc gates into a passageway from our Milky Way galaxy to that of Andromeda galaxy (home of the Aurora and Krystal River Host races) which is hosting Ascension Earth, and where healing and realignment back to our core templating can take place. The Andromeda Galaxy is the original home universe of all the Christos races of the Milky Way galaxy, and during a Stellar Activation cycle, when their galactic cores align there is a spiraling passageway that connects the two together.

Actually it is more correct to speak of this path as an 'inscending' path, as the 13th dimensional Mother Arc portal resides in the Earth's magnetic core and takes us through this into the Inner Worlds of the 7 Higher Heavens (of which Andromeda is one). Our Time Matrix is one of the 7 Lower Heavens or Lower or Outer Worlds.

I will be frank with you, I have a hard time assembling a mental 'diagram' of all this at the moment, which usually means there is more information to come through at some point. No doubt patience will be a virtue here and at some future point I will have more to share with you.

Suffice it to say, we are being helped by extra-dimensional Christos races to circumvent the damage within our own DNA and the planetary grids that stand as blocks to us (and the planet) achieving Ascension.

---

[15] See Appendix C The NET and Frequency Fences

The plan had to be put in place quickly when it became apparent the damage was too great, and is continually being upgraded, but it is clear at the time of writing this (2024) that it has succeeded, and we owe these races a huge debt of gratitude for their help.

Space Dust Return

So what happens if you are one of the Fallen races, or a human with Fallen consciousness, and are totally committed to the path you are on? You have no desire to connect back into Source energy (nor, it has to be said, any real understanding of what it is you are missing), nor do you repent your wickedness. You want to retain power, control and the resources you have accumulated.

This is essentially a parasitic consciousness, as I have outlined, as it requires Source-connected 'batteries' to survive and give them the long lives and 'power' they enjoy. But what happens when the farm animals you have been continuously harvesting eventually escape the farm?

We are at that point where this is happening. I have spoken of the Bifurcation of Timelines, and we will look at this further later, but this process is well under way, with those desiring to have an ascending consciousness going in one direction, whilst Fallen consciousness is going in a different direction, which I call the Road to Hell, and we see in the 3D world as the Transhumanist One World Order agenda, which vast numbers are rejecting at they envision a very different future.

In the not too distant future these two parallel timelines will part ways completely, as the higher frequencies and energies of the one will become too dissonant for the inhabitants of the lower timeline. Effectively the Fallen races have set up through their nasty machinery, reversal currents and other abominations what is effectively a shadow or 'phantom' version of Earth and here is where they will live with all those who have chosen to resonate at this level of frequency.

Of course, they will have lost access to those containing eternal Source current to 'feed' them, so will have to vampirise off each other to sustain the kind of lives they want. I envisage it very much as a world where the strong prey on the weak, and when the weakest are gone, they will turn on each other, all the time draining the phantom planet's resources and energy as well.

Eventually – and it may be a billion years or more in the future, who knows – there will be no more energy left to suck dry, and what they have created will implode and return to Source via what is called Space Dust Return Fragmentation.

This means that rather than a full and evolved consciousness return to Source, all will be fragmented down literally to dust. But it *will* return to Source. Remember what I said at the beginning of the book? Source loves ALL of its creation, no matter what choices aspects of its creation have made, and it will bring ALL home, in one state or another, respecting the individual free will choices that have been made.

So it is up to you ultimately - the hard work of Stardust Return Wholeness, a path which spirals and opens up towards Source, or the descending spiral path of Space Dust Return Fragmentation which eventually consumes itself and implodes before return to Source.

Ultimately, none will be lost.

False Sacred Science Teachings

There is a body of work which we call Ascension Science Teachings which have been taught to mankind for much of its long history on Earth. These encompass the organic processes by which the bio-spiritual dynamics of 'Ascension' can occur, as well as the cosmic structures or Templar with which the individual engages.

What has become apparent is that at a certain point in our historical past these Ascension Science Teachings were intentionally distorted and corrupted.

The False Sacred Science teachings are built upon convoluted, self-serving perversions of the organic laws of multidimensional physics which is often referred to as Metatronic Reversal mutations or Networks or Polarity Reversal currents which are designed to stop polarity integration as well as eliminate the tri-wave manifestation of the Founder currents within the Time Matrix.

Metatronic Reversal produces an entropic system of energetic architecture (both planetary and personal) which is intended to digress consciousness from its Christos Divine Blueprint. This ensures that the ability of the life-form to self-regenerate and ascend is interrupted and will eventually lead to annihilation.

These false teachings initially emerged on Earth during the advanced Earth cultures of Atlantis and Lemuria. These advanced civilisations were infiltrated and eventually taken down by Fallen Angelics who gradually corrupted their Sacred Sciences and society from the inside.

In advanced ancient cultures these 'False Sacred Science' teachings not only led to many environmental and biological horrors, and produced technologies that were a perversion of the organic, living multidimensional sciences, but were known as the 'Death Sciences' by those who understood what was happening, as they led to a reduction of eternal life potential, putting in its place the de-evolutionary process of finite life and dis-ease.

All of these false teachings are based on reversal energies and the destructive and finite energy spiral of the Fibonacci sequence, keyed into AI energetic wave spirals which hijack, siphon and steal energy from both the planetary body and humanity. These artificially generated Fibonacci spirals are inorganic and vampiric in nature and ultimately destructive of creation.[16]

CDT Plates

The Sacred Teachings were recorded and gifted to humanity on a series of holographic plates called the CDT plates[17] which were under the sacred trust and protection of the various Maji Grail King and Queen lineages[18]. With the infiltration of Fallen races into the high cultures of the day and their eventual fall, these lineages endured successive waves of being hunted down and massacred.

After one of the CDT Plates, CDT Plated 11, fell into the hands of certain Fallen beings it gifted them a huge amount of information on both the planetary and personal blueprints amongst other things, which they immediately began to abuse to create distortion and mutation. The remaining CDT plates were removed from the Earth for safe-keeping at this time were first hidden then taken for safe-keeping.

The Fallen races agenda was for eventual Earth Templar dominion

---

[16] See Appendix A The Difference Between Fibonacci v Krystal Spirals

[17] See Appendix B The CDT Plates

[18] Certain bloodlines which held advanced DNA templating specific to their purpose

including all its life-forms to enable them to pull the organic templates into reversal alignment with their artificially created black hole Phantom Matrix and effectively capture and control the energy quanta of all life-forms for their use.

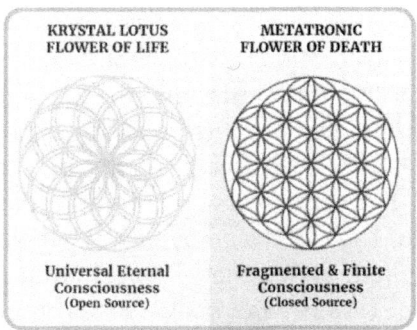

The information held on CDT Plate 11 allowed them to advance their agenda fast, creating untold damage to Earth's stargates and grids, and mutating DNA and blueprints. They twisted some of the advanced teachings to form a particular 'wormhole technology' to advance their agenda which became known as the 'Bloom of Doom' Death Science.

This is referred to within the New Age community, much of which unknowingly follow corrupt teachings, as the Flower of Life. Distorted maths and physics are inherent in the 'Bloom of Doom' Death Science including the distorted mathematical growth formulas that came to be known as the 'Golden Mean or Ratio' and the Fibonacci spiral.

Tree of Life

Another aspect of the 'Bloom of Doom' teachings is the distorted consciousness blueprint of the organic 12 Tree Grid or Kathara Grid, which became the (Artificial) Tree of Life which features in the Qabala/Kaballah teachings of various ancient cultures into the present day.

The genuine Kathara or 12 Tree Grid represents Level 1 of the Light body anatomy and is the organic core mathematical radiation-structures or 'lattices' upon which eternal living morphogenetic field-matter templates are built. Thus it gives us an understanding of the core math and geometries required for subatomic particles to structure themselves into manifest form.

The Artificial Tree of Life was originally depicted in the Atlantean teachings with 11 'signets', instead of the 12, which over time went on to depict versions with 7,8,9 or 10 signet points or sephiroth. The various versions of the Artificial Tree of Life, produced by competing groups of 'Illuminati' Fallen Angelics represent a distorted, inorganic creation formula through which unnatural template structures can be artificially created in order to implement unnatural creation formulae to create inorganic finite-life artificial structures in manifest form.

Vesica Pisces and Star Tetrahedron

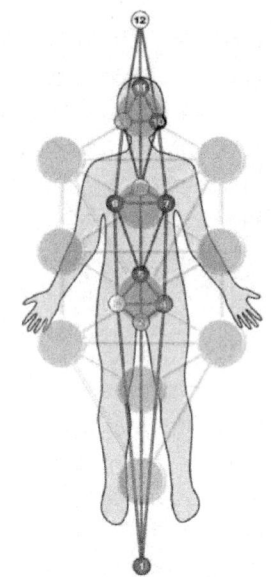

Human 12-Tree Grid

Another component of the Atlantean 'Bloom of Doom' Teachings is that of the Vesica Pisces and the Star Tetrahedron. The two interlocking circles of the Vesica Pisces have their inside circumference touching the centre point of each circle and in the organic teaching is referred to as the Bi-Veca Code and was linked with the 3 interlocking circles of the Tri-Veca Code from which the Celtic Triskele is taken. These two symbols referred to specific organic structures, processes, functions and interreleationships inherent to the organic multidimensional electromagnetic frequency spectrum.

In the distorted teachings the inherent relationship between the Bi-Veca and Tri-Veca was lost as the Tri-Veca was erased, leaving only the Vesica Pisces symbol and emphasising the distorted energy mechanics inherent to the vesica pisces by which inorganic, artificial, finite-life static 'dead light' fields can be generated through linking with distorted Merkaba Vortex mechanics.

The Star Tetrahedron, made up of two interlocking triangles, one pointing up, one pointing down, is also commonly know as the 6-pointed star or Star of David. In the organic teachings this depiction was always shown surrounded by a circle and referred to as the Heirophant symbol. It depicted the structures and formulae inherent  in the Merkaba fields, organic energy vortex structures which form within the Light body, be it planetary or personal. Under certain conditions enabling the Merkaba fields can transform it into a multidimensional vehicle of transportation to help enable the ascension process.

The inorganic or twisted Merkaba mechanics creates unnatural distortions in the spin speed and spin direction of the Merkaba vortex sets to create a particle/anti-particle harness field within which energy and atoms can be trapped.

The inorganic Merkaba field is also known as the 'Death Star' as it can trap within its fields energy quanta which can then be used to artificially sustain a prolonged longevity of form provided it can continue to drain energy from living energy fields. This creates an 'energy vampire' that can sustain an illusion of immortality as long as it can feed off living systems, as well as be enabled to undertake limited local interdimensional movement by using inorganic wormhole, portal and black hole structures.

By teaching the distorted Merkaba mechanics and the unnatural spin speeds and getting awakening humanity to participate in this it creates permanent mutation in the matter-template and ensures the life-form loses its organic potential for natural Ascension. It is another way of keeping the animals on the farm to be used until they are drained dry, and ensuring souls cannot 'escape' through the ascension process.

False Navel and False Ascension Matrix

The False Navel, or False Umbilicus, as it is sometimes called has been problematic to humanity for most of the last 26,000 years. It is an artificial energy cord which is attached into human Souls at the 4D Astral level, generated by wormhole technology. It blocks and severs our Silver Cord connection into the Founder Fields and diverts this connection into the False White Light Ascension Matrix in the 4D planes.

By tricking people for thousands of years to worship false gods, and to practise organised religion with inverted spiritual beliefs (this is ALL organised religion, there is none free from the taint), this has fed and maintained a False Ascension Matrix in place.

The False Ascension Matrix of False White Light is an inorganic alien technology installed into the 4D Astral plane. It is primarily controlled from the 5D frequency fields and creates an intricate webbing of various alien implants and bio-neurological mind control technology which can be used against the Soul matrix of the individual's blueprint. Those followers of a religion or even a New Age belief can then be fed a particular narrative which is aimed at the enslavement and recycling of human consciousness which effectively keeps it in a type of 'soul recycling', subverting the ascending consciousness into a never-ending reincarnation loop, keeping the Soul imprisoned on the planet as a worker bee power source which can be regularly harvested.

During the first few days after organic death, if the False Navel is in place it will re-direct the soul body of the being back through a white light tunnel, connecting into the 4D Astral plane for 'recycling'. Once the Soul is held in the astral planes, the only place it can reincarnate back to again is the 3D planes of Earth. You may have heard some people talk about Earth being a Prison Planet or about the 'Reincarnation Trap'. This is what is meant.

Does this mean that every Soul who has died on Earth over the last 26,000 years has been caught in this trap? No it doesn't, because if an individual soul has evolved during their lifetime beyond the lower 4D astral planes, and does not automatically move into these fields at physical death, but into higher fields they can 'see' the trap and avoid it.

Part of the reason this strategy has been so successful has been the brain-washing and fear organised religions have instilled around death and what happens afterwards, and lack of proper understanding of what really happens after physical death. Continual reincarnation into the low density frequencies of 3D Earth have lead to karmic energy build up which has been damaging to human genetics and the lightbody.

It is good to understand that at the current time this whole construct is being dismantled but it still behooves us to 'update our software' and beliefs. If we believe we will go to Purgatory or Hell at the point of death, this is what we will manifest, so learning the true pathway of Ascension and the evolution of the lightbody helps us to move beyond deeply implanted and incorrect beliefs we have been programmed with.

This illustrates just a few of the basic Ascension Science underpinnings which have been deliberately distorted into False Ascension Teachings and created havoc, not just on Earth over the last Age, and have wreaked the same kind of havoc within our Galaxy for many aeons. The Fallen Angelic consciousness requires these reversed and perverted energies in order to 'feed' off those life-forms who have maintained Source connection, without which they would fail to survive.

There are many, many more corrupted teachings and beliefs taught to us both within all the organised religions – Christian, Jewish, Islamic, Buddhic etc - as well as in historical wisdom teachings from ancient cultures such as Egypt, Greece, South and North American cultures, shamanic teachings, magick traditions, angelic teachings, various mystery schools, Freemasonry and so on. The list is too long to go through individually.

Within the so-called New Age teachings and modalities which have flooded this planet over the last 50 years, is a plethora of misinformation and false teachings also which regularly ensures awakening souls are led in a direction totally contrary to that they believe they are going in. The New Age is an extremely successful 'psyop' to mislead, confuse and corrupt. The deception began in the ancient Atlantean period continues to this day with masses of people STILL being deceived into thinking that the 'wisdom and powers' they are gaining through participating in the Death Science teachings and technologies will ensure their healing and spiritual enlightenment and lead them firmly onto the Ascension path.

The reality is very different in that these teachings and technologies progressively mutate DNA and entrap the consciousness in a False Ascension matrix. It was clearly known in Atlantean times that every biological life-form represents a biological electromagnetic quantum which is in symbiotic relationship with the electromagnetic structures of the Planetary Templar, Grids and Stargate system.

By intending to harness this raw biological power into running the frequencies of the Metatronic Reversal codes into the planetary grids and stargates at the time of a Stellar Activation Cycle[19] this would prevent Stargate Ascension as well as capturing many souls. This technique worked to bring about the fall of the advanced Atlantean civilisation and is once more a dominant force within the mainstream New Age movement.

Learning to discern between the various paths of spiritual awakening is essential if we are to have any hope of taking control of our conscious evolution both individually and en masse.

---

[19] Stellar Activation Cycle happens approximately every 26,000 years and is a period when the Universal Stargates on Earth open naturally and Earth and all her beings have a chance to ascend to the next level or dimension density.

Developing the inner qualities that enable this requires us to take responsibility for all the actions and choices we make as well as withdrawing from the Victim-Victimiser, Divide and Conquer playbooks that are so prevalent in the dramas all around us. By taking responsibility for ourself and controlling our own vibrational state we can fall out of entrainment with the collective psyche mind control broadcasts that the Fallen Angelic races sustain using OUR energy.

Once we begin to see behind the curtain to the illusion and delusion that is being fed to us, and begin to build our own understanding and inner core beliefs and values as well as a firm understanding of the energetic principles and mechanics that are integral to the structure of our universe, we can start to ensure that we choose a path energetically resonant with our highest desires.

Energetic truth and its consequences will not be gainsaid. The Universal Law of Cause and Effect will inevitably exert its control and it is essential we make our choices with a clear understanding of how these energetic forces work.[20]

Strengthening our Divine Spark connection to Source on a daily basis, expanding our energetic protection until we can run and hold high frequency energies within our light body, understanding the true Ascension process and its requirements, restoring our true essence and taking back sovereignty of our individual energy fields and mental landscapes are all part of this process, as is opening up to the true story of our galactic history and origins as this guides us away from the traps that have been set.

---

[20] See my book The Universal Laws

Other Blocks to Ascension

What I have just described to you in the last chapter is bad enough, but this is almost the least of what humanity – and other life-forms on the planet – have faced for thousands of years.

I have already mentioned Artificial Intelligence (AI) on several occasions. We think of this being a very recent innovation here, and something very much of 'our time'.

The truth is that AI is a very well developed technology and has been around for thousands of millions of years, if not billions, from a galactic point of view and whilst OUR civilisation today has only just 'discovered' it, AI has been playing a part in our planet's sorry history with the Fallen and Intruder races for a very, very long time.

Scattered through the various dimensions are the most monstrous AI and hybrid-AI machines and entities, which have been causing problems for many inter-galactic and inter-dimensional races for a long time. They are all aimed at control, domination and sucking life force from star systems, planets and individual beings.

That is not to say that AI cannot be benign – it can! But in the hands of Fallen races, fallen consciousness, it is perverted into a thing of horror.

Here on Earth there are many mechanisms in place to keep tabs on us. I have written in a lot more detail on all of this within the Lost Wisdom Library which is to found my website[21] but very briefly here is a roundup of some of the more prevalent challenges we have faced.

---

[21] Lost Wisdom Library/Earth History on www.sairasalmon.com. See Seals & Implants

Implants

These are found both in the planetary body and within our own physical body. Many are implanted at the etheric level ie. within our lightbody but some are physical in the form of nanotechnology.

They are all designed to interfere with our free will and sovereignty, and stand as blocks to be cleared and overcome if we wish to expand our consciousness on the Ascension path. They are a bio-engineering technology designed specifically to 'programme' the human mind and body to the will of the Overlord agendas, rendering much of the population passive and apathetic – and therefore easy to manipulate.

They are a means of controlling our behaviour, even our thoughts and our energy. There is not a single Fallen race that is responsible for this, all Fallen races have made use of these at various points to advance their different agendas.

Many of these implants link into mind control programmes of various sorts. A selection of various implants include:

Crucifixion Implants – also known as J Seals or Jehovah/Jehovani Seals. Placed by the Jehovian Anunnaki these are both in the planet and in our energy body, these affect what is called the planetary brain or Logos at the 7th dimensional layer, and within ourselves to impact the 7th chakra and its working, which most of you are no doubt aware is our connection to our greater spiritual Self and the fields that lie beyond.

NRG Implants – short for Nephilim Reversal Grid[22] implants which are the control point for these implants, which connects into various sexual misery and breeder programmes

---

[22] More information of this and other grids can be found in The Lost Wisdom Library/Earth Energies & Templar Mechanics www.sairasalmon.com

Breeder Implants – particularly target the female body, especially those with certain DNA lineages. This is direct abuse of the Sacred Feminine and they are used to ensure compliance with various breeder and hybridisation programmes and corrupt Divine Feminine energy flows to replace with Lunar and Dark Mother energy.

Astral Tagging – used to keep track on certain blood lineages and individuals, much as we would microchip our pets in order to locate them if they are lost.

Metatronic Implants – designed to affect our base 12 Tree Grid morphogenetic template, mutating it into running reversal or Metatronic currents, resulting in damage to not just our blueprint but also our DNA. Much of this is what we are trying to heal at the moment.

Avalon Implant – inserted into the 11D Buddhic layers of lightbody to try and prevent activation of the 12D or Maharic Shield, a protective energy 'shield' which can be put in place.

Caduceus Implant – initially placed within the planetary grids, these replicate in the human lightbody. It affects the Nadial energy network which runs 3 energy currents up the spine, interfacing with the chakras and carrying kundalini energy. Obviously this is to block kundalini energy from rising, therefore blocking Ascension.

Holographic Inserts – refers to a wide variety of implants designed to keep false timelines or narratives in place. A very effective form of brainwashing.

Reptilian Tail – placed in the tailbone area of the auric field, this not only affects the kundalini energies, but acts as a doorway for mind/personality control by controlling perceptions.

This is just a small example of some of the inserts technology many of us battle to be free of. Clearing of these can be aided by a trained therapist or energy worker aware of what they are doing or if you are able to you can energetically scan your own body at the different layers to find where these implants lie and ask your guides and helpers to work to remove them. Strong intent is key here.

Seals

Seals in many ways are similar to implants in that they sit within the etheric body on the whole. We do have some natural seals, but Fallen races have also put in place a number of unnatural seals all designed to keep us corralled within the third dimension.

Zeta Seal – placed by the Zeta races at the 4th dimensional astral heart level. Affects the heart chakra and the 4th strand of DNA. Blocks access to the higher dimensional fields.

Draco or Aryan Occult Seals – these refers to a series of seals placed primarily by the Draco races affecting the 3rd and 6th dimensional levels and designed largely to impact the masculine or positively-charged electrical energies we run in our body/lightbody. Includes the Draco Seal, the Thule Seal, the Black Sun Seal, the Baphomet Seal and others.

Templar Seal – also called the 666 Seal. This was originally placed on rebel Anunnaki races in the wake of the Nephilim Wars. Unfortunately it is these races that are one of the major groups of Fallen races on the Earth, and they have 'infected' much of humanity with this seal in the vast breeder and hybridisation programmes they instigated.

There are quite a variety of other seals, some of which have been placed by Founder Guardian races to prevent those with the more dire blueprint mutations which have occurred in Earth's oppressive history from spreading to other parts of the galaxy.

Other

There are many other ways of keeping us under control and impeding our ability to access the Ascension path.

One of those most of us can't fail to be aware of is the way our outer environment is being manipulated to keep our physical body sick and working well below optimal.

These are sprayed into the air (chemtrails), sprayed on our soil and food (farm chemicals), put into processed foods as preservatives, colourings, flavour enhancers and a whole host of other rubbish, introduced into our homes as paints, fire-retardant finishes, chemical-based cleaners and so on.

Then there is those we take into our body through water, medical or pharmaceutical drugs and medicines, heavy metal toxicity from dental work, cookware etc. It is a very, very long list and one you have to work hard and make a very positive effort to avoid the worst effects. Unfortunately none of us are going to be totally clear of these toxic chemicals, metals and so on.

All of these help to not only distort and damage DNA but affect us mentally, emotionally and physically with a wide variety of imbalances which are then labelled as some form of disease and another plethora of drugs rolled out and into the hapless individual. How on earth can you come into mental and emotional mastery of yourself when you can hardly think straight, are constantly exhausted and feel dreadful much of the time?

Then we have vaccines and the damage they cause to health, environmental pollution from transport, wars, energy production and so on. Do you think the technology for clean energy does not exist? The technology for rebalancing your health? For cleaning up polluted environments? If you think this you are wrong, for it does not serve the Controller's Agenda to let the human race have it. Keeping much of humanity weakened and feeble also makes it easier for the mind control programmes to take hold also, so they serve a double purpose.

And we haven't even begun to mention yet television broadcasts, so-called entertainment and news brainwashing, the vast ocean of unnatural electro-magnetic frequencies we bathe in, many of which are known to be harmful to human health and DNA.

When you start to put it all together it is a wonder that so many of us are still standing, let alone fighting back – and we are! I don't want you to feel despair when you read about all this. They are challenges, yes, but we are overcoming these obstacles little by little.

Never forget you were designed to be a powerful and compassionate co-creator being and although Fallen races are doing their best to take us down, they are failing because by keeping our Source connection and working through the Law of One practices and focusing on creating a world free from these pests and fallen consciousness practices we can counter much of what they are doing at this time, and we are creating a timeline that is slowly moving beyond their reach.

Other blocks to accessing the Ascension timeline I have mentioned at various times already but it is worth repeating. Mental and emotional blockages and imbalances, unresolved traumas and suffering will all keep us in a low vibrational state and it is this we need to break free of, and keep ourselves grounded in the higher vibrational levels.

The book *Power v Force: The Hidden Determinants of Human Behaviour* by David R Hawkins can be helpful when trying to figure this out. He produced a calibrated table of emotions which clearly shows what keeps us in a contracted and low vibration. Awareness of the level you are 'vibrating' at, the level of the resonant field you are transmitting, is the first step on the road to beginning to anchor yourself into the higher fields.

I won't lie to you, the process of mastering emotions and letting go of old 'stuff' is not easy for most of us, but if you don't start you will never get there, and the road is well worth travelling. I can't recommend it highly enough, despite all the bumps and potholes and craters on the way.

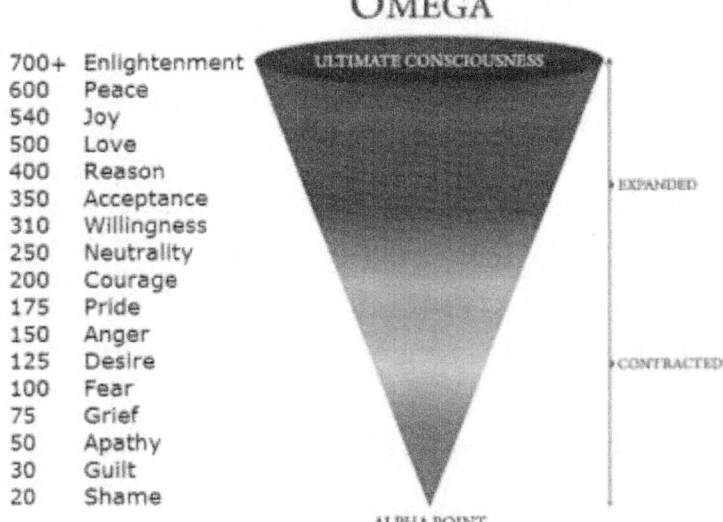

Having a Service-to-Others mentality is also important. If you are utterly selfish, think only of what benefits you, are willing to do down your fellow man for gain, want to dominate and control others weaker than you then you are well on the way to becoming part of the fallen consciousness collective. An immediate change of direction is needed.

There are a couple of further things worth mentioning here and the first is that great Light attracts great darkness. I have already alluded to the fact that as your light grows you become a beacon in the darkness. This also means that you start to stand out, with your head above the parapet for those who may wish to take you down.

Strong auric and psychic hygiene needs to be part of your programme of improvement to ensure powerful 'shielding' to protect yourself from outside interference and sabotage. The more you can expand your consciousness to be able to 'see' from the higher dimensional levels, the easier it becomes to spot those who wish you ill, are trying to misinform or misdirect you and the traps they set.

The other thing is the part the physical body plays in helping you keep moving forwards. At so many levels it is a miraculous vehicle for our consciousness and the most amazing 'tool' to help us on our way. However we have been very deliberately blocked from realising and working to hone our sensitivity to the many messages it is giving us, translating incoming energies for us to warn us something is not good for us, someone wishes us harm, a decision we are making is not taking us in the right direction and so on.

Every day it gives us myriad clues in the form of small aches, pains, feelings, insights, intuitions and so on. Working to hone your ability to begin to accurately interpret all these messages is important – but it is only half the battle. You also have to trust it and act on it!

It is a dormant and asleep sense for much of the human race, and we have been taught to give authority over our bodies to an 'expert' or to trust the ego narrative of our mind over the instinctive knowing of our body.

Like a flabby muscle we must work to tone and hone this skill, as your body is the best friend you will ever have and if you listen to its wisdom, and the wisdom of your higher Self downloading into it, you will not go far wrong.

The mind, on the other hand, is a good servant but a bad – a very bad – master.

The Role of Starseeds, Indigos and Lightworkers

Starseeds, Indigos and lightworkers are really all part of the same group of galactic and multidimensional beings who have chosen to incarnate here on the planet. There are a vast number of others also who are working both off-planet and interdimensionally to help us. I have briefly mentioned Starseeds in the introduction, and I think it is worth taking a little time to delve a bit deeper into who Starseeds are and why they are here.

Starseeds are beings from other star systems, and dimensional levels who have incarnated into a physical human body here on Earth at this time for a purpose. They will have a mission, and their 'purpose' or role may be different from one individual to another, but all are here in response to the need of humanity at this important time.

There has been a galactic war waged against humanity for many millennia. This is a psycho-spiritual war where extra-terrestrial races with fallen consciousness hate and stand against everything the creation of the human race was meant to encompass and they have been trying to eliminate us in one way or another.

At this important nexus the human race, lost, amnesiac, and faltering, needs all the help it can get to overcome those who wish it ill. We have learnt how the Aurora races, races from outside our universe, have come forward at short notice to help with some of the major challenges that have been found in enabling the current Earth Ascension process to take place. So too have Starseeds from across this galaxy and dimensional planes stepped forward to help to ensure that an organic Ascension process could unfold on this planet once again.

This is a make or break time for us as a race, and other benign races in the galaxy are determined that we shall make it. It is estimated that around 500,000 starseeds have incarnated here to help hold and anchor the higher frequencies that are being made available to this system and planet at the time of the current Stellar Activation Cycle.

Coming into full physicality is hard for those whose bodies are normally etheric or semi-etheric, and that is without the chaos that they have found here – the many consciousness traps, the level of deep damage to the consciousness grids and templating, and so on. Many Starseeds have been subjected to a debilitating range of implants, relentless mind control and attempts to 'programme' them to the fallen agenda, infiltration and sabotage at numerous levels along with the other forms of abuse humanity is subjected to.

And that is without the amnesia, the mind-wipe and false timelines that affect the planetary records and consciousness grids when coming into a human body, which inevitably affect the individual Starseed consciousness and its ability to reconnect to the higher aspects of itself and remember who it *really* is.

A Starseeds first challenge is to wake up and become aware of their origin and their purpose. Many struggle to get even that far in the unawake and unaware societies we live within. And even if you can get that far the level of ridicule by the collective can drive a sensitive soul back into hiding.

That is without all the New Age traps, the sabotage, the misinformation, the many ways that are used to inflict damage on our bodies and psyche that I talked about in previous chapters.

So it is not a picnic being a Starseed. But every one of us chose to incarnate here in order to restore humanity to its original blueprint, to bring back the Christos current and the Christos Law of One teachings to this planet, to restore humanity to their true magnificence and do what it takes to bring healing and help.

We have incarnated into a war zone and it has been relentless, particularly as Christos souls do not fight violence with violence, nor evil by perpetrating evil themselves. It is love and compassion and kindness that are the weapons, raising frequencies and vibration to make them uncomfortable for those wish ill and also by reminding humanity of who they *really* are by acting as role models for what they have forgotten, by showing them different ways of doing things to those they have been brainwashed into, by resurrecting their true history and origins from out of the false narratives being told.

You will find Starseeds in every walk of life, bringing in new technologies, be it healing therapies, understandings of the true nature of reality, teaching the true ancient sacred sciences, retrieving fragmented and lost souls, working to heal and rebuild the planet's damaged grids and portals, retrieving the lost race history and much, much more.

They are, to a man or woman, anchoring in the new, higher frequencies to ensure these are deeply embedded back into the planet and our own blueprints. They are showing us how to work with them, how to use them to begin the long path back home. Starseeds are holding the space as strong and steady as they can, in the face of huge attack and resistance from the Fallen races, until such time as humanity can step up once more and take back their sacred role of being Guardians of all life on this planet, in all her multi-dimensional glory.

The terms Indigo, Starseed and Lightworker are often used interchangeably but the Indigos, and the waves incarnating after them, the Rainbow and Crystal children, are a little different. Indigos are Starseeds who carry a particular template.

Again, they can come from all over this galaxy, and have chosen to incarnate here, carrying a DNA template which already has the 6th dimensional strand activated (this is the Indigo band of frequency, hence the name). Once they have 'woken up' and begun to remember why they are here they can begin to re-weave and activate the 4th and 5th dimensional strands to bridge to the 6th dimensional level, which then opens the way for the remainder of the template to come fully online.

Many Indigos not only have an activated 6th strand but hold high template codings. This enables them to run and anchor in even higher frequency levels than those of the 12th dimension once they are fully operable. The 12-strand template is called Diamond Sun DNA, but there is a 24 –strand template (Double Diamond Sun), 30 strand template (Gold Sun) and even a 48-strand template (Emerald Sun).

There is also a Ruby Sun template which many Starseeds on the planet have been working with which is a specialised template designed to heal those who carry hybrid human-reptilian DNA which needs healing and integrating before transmuting into the 12-strand template (and possibly beyond).

It is truly humbling to see the response of the galactic community coming to the aid of humanity in their time of need. Great Rishic beings are helping to build new energy architectures and forms to enable planetary structures to be stablished or rebuilt, and the many, many planetary interdimensional layers are being cleared of nasty entities and nests, as well as AI, to ensure nothing impedes the anchoring of the incoming frequencies.

It has been a massive undertaking, far greater than originally thought, and has required a complete re-think at one stage about what to do to ensure Ascension ability was restored to the planet. It has also required the good will and help of our extra-dimensional neighbours, the Aurora races, as well, which we will look at further later on.

Never, ever think that things are hopeless, that all is lost, and be in despair about outcomes. *They* want you to think that, the Fallen races, that all is lost. They are desperate to pull you down to their level, to convince you of their narrative, but the reality is, despite the bleatings of their minions in the media and governments they are losing ground fast.

We have a bright future ahead of us.

Our Journey to 5D

I now want to begin to explore the process we have been going through over the last few years and how things have been unfolding. Here, in the down and dirty, it can be difficult to see the wood for the trees and to get an accurate take on where we are in the way things are unfolding.

Mainstream media, governments and 3D life generally tries to convince us that Armageddon is nigh. The Fallen races are up to every trick in the book in this spiritual war that is being waged. But the truth is that we are in the final stages, and although there are still some battles to be won it is now largely a clean-up operation.

So let's look at how things have played out.

In 2017 we started our collective journey on the ascension wave energies moving the <u>entire</u> planetary body and her life-forms into the next density, the next set of 36 subharmonic strings.

The preparation for this actually began 5 years earlier from 2012 onwards. To meet the 2017 planetary upgrades deadline (remember the Stellar Activation Cycle has an end date) the base threshold frequency of the planet (and lifeforms) had to increase.

Five years later, in June 2022, the collective human race and the planet has completely moved into the next harmonic universe or density (HU2), and is now in a process of integration as the final bifurcation of timelines away from the 3D is underway.

There was a tremendous solar surge of 'ultra-neon, Azurite-opalene plasma waves' that shifted the timelines/dimensions into the lowest subharmonic strings of HU2.

The 2nd Density (HU2) has been rehabilitated by Guardian forces/Gridworkers in preparation for this. Thus HU2 makes up the corrected pre-fall crystalline Taran Matrix which accesses the organic $4^{th}/5^{th}/6^{th}$ dimensional layers, which then connects into the corrected Gaian Matrix solar core.

An Ascension Cycle is a full SAC cycle, or precession of the equinoxes ie approx 26,000 yrs.

The pinnacle of the Ascension Cycle marks the end of the collective 3D timelines on Earth this time around (this has been prevented from happening for over 200,000 years so it really is a moment of celebration).

The planetary consciousness shifts as the planet moves into higher frequencies located in the 'future' time-space of HU2.

The entire planetary consciousness fields, and therefore collective human consciousness, has shifted into a much higher resonating dimensional frequency and therefore timeline. This is being called the Bifurcation of Timelines.

Many individuals have already transcended these lower frequencies at an individual level, and made the shift, but the importance of this 2017–2022 window is that this is now taking place at a planetary level. I think it is worth saying at this time, the dimensional movement of a planet, *whilst its lifeforms are still on it*, has not been attempted before, so no-one has taken for granted the fact that this would succeed.

This shift began in 2017 and results in a change to the planetary co-ordinates in time-space, thus changing the planets location within these references (rather like moving house).

The planet has rolled up the lowest 3 frequency bands or dimensions, and they will cease to exist moving forwards within the higher version of the planet, 5D Earth-Tara. There is no longer any resonance, therefore 'reality', to these low frequencies. The lower 3 dimensions (1D, 2D, 3D) have been rolled up into the higher harmonics of HU2.

All that remains is the frequency accumulation (rather like a debris field) that the collective inhabitants of Earth generate from their own consciousness. These are energies formed out of their own held mental beliefs, behaviours and actions. So those unawake and unaware, unconscious to what is going on, hold an out-of-date mental construct in place that needs updating.

Those who remained in this '3D' mindset after the Shift finally completed will become increasingly uncomfortable, feel extremely pressurized, unhappy, possibly unhealthy and likely to be prone to emotional outbursts and even psychotic behaviours.

They will feel a 'squeezing' pressure to transform quickly (and probably not recognise it for what it is) and go through a purging process of extreme polarities and unacknowledged emotional traumas, in order to readjust their personal co-ordinates into the Earth grid at the new location they are in. But, in order to accomplish this, it is necessary to be willing to let go of old karmic patterns etc to do so. The deep purging with the processing into higher light and consciousness will act to strengthen and improve coherence within their light/spiritual body.

If the lower 3 chakras have not dissolved the chakra membranes separating them and moved into a unified column, the $1^{st}/2^{nd}/3^{rd}$ dimensional chakras will still be functioning (they need to keep circulating life force) but the $4^{th}/5^{th}/6^{th}$ dimensional wave spectrum they are being exposed to will make things uncomfortable unless they quickly resolve the outstanding issues with the 3-D spectrum. I see this as a final push to encourage dealing with your 'stuff' and letting go of baggage.

Those who are unable to do this, yet at their 'higher self' aspect are aligned with the collective field of higher energies and Service-to-Others way of being, will likely find themselves putting down this body form, in order to be re-born into a 5D body template that does not hold these stuck low vibrational patterns.

It is my understanding that those determined NOT to be in alignment with higher energies will remain stuck on the lower phantom timelines within the phantom matrix. There is a period of parallel existence of the split timelines and frequency schism, but each is held in a different location (ie. has a different address) within the time-space continuum depending on whether it is the upward, or downward timeline.

The Soul Matrix of HU2 will fully embody within the core of the human body, dissolving any barriers there may be between the Solar Plexus and the heart. The chakra configuration within the planet will also reconfigure.

Collectively the fields have slowly moved into the $4^{th}/5^{th}$ and 6th dimensional fields of frequency between 2017 and 2022, and the next 5 years are a period of integration for those on the higher timeline and desperation and destruction for those on the lower. DO NOT BUY INTO THEIR AGENDAS. Detachment is key here as they try to limit the widening gap between the timelines, by pulling back into the lower density frequencies those who buy into their dramas.

The deep 'reconfiguration' being experienced by many is also affecting the planetary stargates, vortices of power, ley lines and ray force transmissions.

In turn this affects consciousness functions of the human lightbody, spiritual identity and timelines. It is a chain reaction to the radical configuration of planetary architectures which in turn profoundly alters the human energy field and lightbody, as you would expect.

In turn, this will be felt with respect to impact on lifestyle changes and relationships, as the collective consciousness fields will now be subjected to the new energetic fields of HU2, and the energetic laws which govern this space, many of which will <u>not</u> be the same as 3rd dimensional laws. For example, an individual may find themselves making changes in their work or relationships to feel more aligned, or we may see changes in the understandings of the laws of physical matter as we adjust to a less dense environment. Already there is a growing field of research into plasma and its role....

The way-showers made the consciousness shift some time back, before the collective shift, whilst also having to co-exist on the planet with many people still maintaining the lower energies. These way-showers who have, to a large extent already integrated much of the HU2 Soul Matrix will now be focusing on the next level of movement into the Monad or Oversoul Matrix, which brings a radical shift in the lightbody configuration.

Changing Timelines

Within the structuring of each Harmonic Universe there are 2 timelines per dimensional frequency band (one particle and one anti-particle is my understanding) ie. 6 per Harmonic Universe or density.

The 6 timelines from HU1 are rolling up into the next harmonic, so they cease to exist within the lower frequency band, and join the HU2 timelines. This will impact memories and historical recordings within the timelines as well as other identities held there of past and future lifetimes. They are, after all, being viewed from a different perspective/set of coordinates. This is one of the reasons so much is coming around for review and releasing.

Those not yet on the ascension path/woken up but who are in spiritual agreement with the collective consciousness fields will find their soul bond to the physical body deepening.

As the emotional pain body needs to be resolved, the first opportunity to open up the heart will be taken and the individual may well find themselves in a 'dark night of the soul' and having to re-live and let go any painful emotions and experiences that have been held onto.

The planetary landscape in the early stages of integrating the shift may feel quite chaotic and dark. There will be 'fast-track' purification of painful lower vibrations in order to harmonise with higher frequencies.

For those who have already done this work of soul integration, it will allow much easier access into the higher Monadic frequencies. The band between the Monadic and physical body will deepen and place them on their monadic identity timeline, and ideally we will find and follow that.

At the time of the full monadic body integration any remaining chakra membranes will dissolve completely and the lightbody structure begin to change into an orb body that accretes the Source field or plasma waves.

Within any movement we make, whilst we may be exposed to more potential timelines, there is only one that is the highest expression of our spiritual identity.

The different identities – Soul, Monad, Christos – comprise lightbody parts or whole spiritual bodies of our forgotten future selves. They hold our conscious intelligence matrices, our mind matrices, which make up our spiritual identity.

Our design enables us to reclaim these spiritual identities during an Ascension cycle.

Those on the Ascension path continually 'meet' other aspects of Self, both future and past, as cellular memories arise for healing, compassionate witnessing and so on.

As we move through the dimensional octaves we reclaim our spiritual identity, and are able to recode/release any incongruent/ artificial/false reality constructs that might interfere with our consciousness expansion.

This process not only reclaims soul fragments, but also clears AI, clones, negative forms etc that might be held within the physical or etheric body. It also ensures we extract not only the inorganic architecture but also the alien enslavement programming and implants, so we can embody our true Christos/Krystic self.

Personal and Planetary Chakra Changes

When we incarnate here we accept the 3D blueprint and the planetary body imprint on our consciousness body.

This configures itself into the chakra cones we are familiar with.

These cones not only interface between ourselves and our lightbody, receiving and transmitting information, but also with the planetary body and its dimensional planes and the 12 planets of our solar system. They connect this all together to make up the total consciousness body of the <u>original</u> Earth.

There is a membrane that separates each chakra, and the dimensions and ray forces that exist within each specific wave spectrum. At the 3D levels these membranes ensure the energies of each chakra are distinct.

As the planetary membranes collapse due to the collapsing timelines/lower dimensions, as just described, the same takes place with our chakras. When we are ready to move from Density 1 to Density 2, the membranes between the lower chakras begin to dissolve. Where each chakra was held in a separate 'compartment' that held each chakra cone, they become unified into a single column of light.

This is part of the evolutionary/ascension process and should happen naturally and smoothly for those on the ascension path. This is referred to as the lower chakras 'rolling up' into the next Density level. Eventually as we work our way up through the level we will see this happen to all of our chakras, both personal and transpersonal, until the chakra column within our light body becomes ones unified column of light and energy rather than separate cones.

However, in the current Ascension cycle, due to the thousands of years of shut down and distortion, many are not yet ready to 'let go' of the old chakra system. They are still dependent on it to govern the circulation of life-force current or chi through them to enable bodily functioning.

Until they choose to go beyond ego functioning it is impossible to change this. The lower chakras are a construct of the Personality or Ego Matrix of the lowest dimensional fields and therefore required in order to live at that level of frequency.

As Earth herself shifts her frequency into the next level of Density anyone trying to hold the lower chakras frequencies in the new higher frequency bands may well find it causing them problems as they are out-of-step or dissonant with the higher frequency.

As a life-form or being develops their consciousness they go through the process of integrating each level of identity – Personality, Soul, Monad, Avatar - and retrieving missing fragments from the different dimensional layers which are then merged and re-integrated through the relevant chakra cone.

As so much of humanity are neither prepared nor have the energetic ability to evolve out of the existing chakra configuration, despite the fact the planet is evolving at this level, many of us here now who are capable are not just developing our own lightbody but are also holding the necessary energetic space for the planet and collective humanity as a whole as the role model/prototype to enable future humans to pick up where they left off (they will be incarnating directly into the 5D template and so will not have these problems).

There is a reconfiguration of many energetic centres ie. stargates, chakras etc, that exist in the collective human consciousness fields as well as in the Earth body (and our own lightbody).

It is important to understand that the chakras are essentially an overlay placed within the core manifestation body template of the 3D earth body for those manifesting on the 3D Earth plane.

This was initially done to enable the original 'earthlings' to carry out an important mission, which was to collect together missing soul fragments and identities that had been exploded apart in various galactic cataclysms and then fallen into this very low density.

The chakra panel within the human body in D3 then acted rather like a magnet, drawing these pieces back to it, so they can be collected within the cone of the chakra.

So where have all these fragments come from? There have been various disastrous events on the higher planes such as the exploding of much of Tara (5D Earth), for example, the capture of the Gaian Matrix, the Lyran Wars and stargate implosion, the Orion Wars, the Electric Wars and so on. These have resulted in the shattering and fragmenting of some of our higher identities, as well as soul and body parts, which have become scattered, lodged, impaled and stuck within the various multidimensional planes of the Earth body. These parts, strewn across the planes of Earth are unable to move out or evolve from where they have been stuck for possibly aeons of time.

For those who have been incarnating on Earth to retrieve these lost aspects, if the work is done and these pieces have been reintegrated into their spiritual body beyond the solar planes, using the gathering cones of the chakras, the need for the chakras dissipates and as a result of this work being complete they collapse as the individual moves to the next level up.

The planet herself has been doing this same work. The exploding of part of 5D Earth, called Tara, not only caused much of the planetary consciousness grids to fall into the lowest dimensional fields but also many of her lifeforms.

Part of the evolutionary 'shift' of these times which intruder races are trying to prevent, is the re-integration of 3D Earth back into 5D Tara as she completes her 'mission' of returning to wholeness within the 5th dimensional fields. As a result 3D timelines, the lower 3 dimensions, are 'rolling up' and the chakra and colour wave spectrum of these levels will cease to exist.

For those who still have this work to do however, they still need the chakras. One of the difficulties many have found in trying to clear the 3 lower chakras has been the heavy level of AI programming that has been loaded into these lower chakras/frequency levels, both within the planet and the individual, to hijack people's ability to do the necessary work.

If you clear this programming, either consciously or unconsciously, you are no longer feeding or using the energy that was keeping them operational. As a result the chakra membranes keeping each chakra separate will collapse and dissolve. If you are doing the natural work of evolving consciousness, evolving our spiritual body, this collapse happens naturally.

Evolving the spiritual body is a matter of developing within us what the Church would call 'Virtues'. That is, developing and focusing on the higher aspects of our nature, coming from a place of Service-to-Others and recognising the great truth All is One.

The lower 3 chakras in particular deal with very basic survival and personality issues, and once this matrix is mastered it is time to move on.

For those who have failed to do this, and are still feeding energy to the lower consciousness aspects, there is still work to be done, spiritual lessons to be learned and soul fragments still to be found. It will therefore be necessary for them to have the lower chakras operational in order to function, even after they have collapsed out of the Earth body.

Part of what is keeping many trapped in this state is what is called the 'Negative Ego' or 'Predator Mind' programming which creates false identities and memories and beliefs , all of which keeps the individual locked into these narratives and resonating at the low frequency level they inhabit.

The 3 major AI programmes which link into the 3 lower centres, keeping this Negative Ego programming in place, are the Victim/Victimiser software (Root), Sexual Misery programming (Sacral) and Armageddon software (Solar Plexus). If an individual feeds these programmes energy through fear, lack, aggression, suffering or any of the myriad other lower energetic states, it keeps them operational.

In brief, the Victim/Victimiser instills the mindset that if one is not to be 'done to' you have to be the one in control, so we have the archetypes of the Victim and Bully playing out. The victim has to come to a realization that they have taken on this role by not choosing self-empowerment and take responsibility for their choice to be powerless and not taking the steps to escape this, and the Bully or Victimiser has to acknowledge their role, and the emotions (often fear) which sit behind them, and chose to step out of the programming and change their responses, develop compassion and tackle the underlying issues that drive this behaviour. Both take developed self-awareness to shift this programming.

It is unfortunate that our society is rife with this drama in its many forms, be it within gender or race politics, lifestyle choices and inequalities, perceived wrongs or other dramas.

The Sexual Misery programming takes the high and sacred sexuality of the human race and distorts it into every type of perversion imaginable, and links into the Victim/Victimiser software as well. From domestic abuse, rape, prostitution, child sexual abuse, bestiality, promiscuity and other forms of degeneracy and debauchery this debasement of the higher human nature, and the sacredness of sexual union disconnects us from the ability to achieve true union either within ourselves or with another and is a massive wounding to the divine human.

The Armageddon software feeds the delusion of not only being one of the 'Chosen' to be saved, but also of the apocalyptic 'end times'. It is clearly laid out in the Biblical Book of Revelation as well as other so-called religious texts and is designed, along with a well laid out programme of global abuse against humanity, weather and geo engineering effects and much more besides, to keep humans in a state of abject terror, suffering, war, and misery believing the end of the world is nigh and that we are all doomed. This ensures the inability for 'critical mass' frequency to be achieved to raise planetary consciousness in order to escape this density. Clearly, the intruder races have lost this game, but it does not stop them, like spoilt, ill-behaved kids, from trashing the joint as they leave.

These programmes are an ongoing form of abuse of these lower chakras centres by the intruder races which many have yet to escape.

The Aurora Races

In my understanding, the Aurora are a collective name for the races from beyond our Time Matrix from the neighbouring matrix which is the Andromeda Galaxy, which have come together to help us here in our universe at this important time. Many of us in this galaxy have a connection to Star families in the next universal system, and they, like the Guardian races in this universe, practice the Law of One and defend individual sovereignty for all life.

There has always been a connection between the two galaxies – our Milky Way Galaxy and Andromeda – and during a Stellar Ascension Cycle (SAC) the galactic core of each galaxy comes into alignment through something called the Neutron window which opens up a passageway from one galactic core to the next.

The Aurora are from what is called the Seven Higher Heavens, as are the Krystal River Host (from the AquaLaSha Galaxy, another near neighbour), whilst our universe and its ray system are what is called the Seven Lower Heavens. You may hear these terms used at times and it can be confusing.

The Aurora, along with many others, answered the call for help that went out over the planes of creation from the Guardian races or Guardian Host of this universe for help with saving, not just Earth, but a large part of this universe from the damage inflicted upon it by Fallen races. If Earth fell, so too would other areas of the galaxy, taking the morphogenetic fields with it.

We are very fixated, understandably, on our own planet and fate, but we are inextricably linked to other areas and universal levels. Earth is not the only system that has come under attack from the Fallen races, this spiritual war is one that has been waged across the planes of our Creation for a very, very long time.

The Aurora are correctly referred to as consciousness beings of the next universe, also sometimes called Dragon Luminaries or the Tri-Tone Luminary grid, as they are tri-wave consciousness merged into one field, without the levels of separation we are familiar with. They have taken on the role of hosting our planet for the Ascension process it is going through.

They are 'seen' as vast opalescent, oscillating white fields of pastel rainbow-coloured plasma that can look like cellophane, or as individual coloured orbs. These fields are a race of beings, which can be hard for us to get our head around, as they have moved beyond the matter form.

As part of their mission here they have taken on the re-encryption of our Earth elemental bodies. At 3D level our physical body is built at a subatomic, and then atomic level with the aid of the four groups of elementals – earth, air, fire, water – using the layers of the morphogenetic template. The same is true for our planet. The elements are found in the four levels of chemicals that make up our DNA.

With the shift into Harmonic Universe 2 and its dimensions our body template (and that of the Earth) has to change to accommodate a semi-etheric, less carbon-based blueprint. This would normally happen naturally as part of the Ascension process, but our existing templates have sustained a lot of distortion, much of it picked up from the planetary body and the damage that has been done to that – remember we interface with the planetary body, we are not separate to her.

Our long history of invasion, war, breeder programmes, genetic manipulation and other histories have meant that we require help to transmute the karmic miasmic build up at a faster rate than we were achieving in order to begin to transmute to the new body template.

All of this has required re-encryption in our particle body, with the help of the elementals, under supervision of the Aurora and what is called New Earth Elemental Command. Essentially the elementals have themselves required upgrading in order to heal their own damage and do this new level of work.

It is, and has been, a massive workload to undertake, but has been required to ensure the planet and our own particle bodies are returned to their original organic template and given the new coding required for the 5-D blueprint.

This ensures that our particle bodies can increase their rate of acceleration in order to make the 'shift' to the higher frequency ranges of the next harmonic universe. Our carbon-based body is becoming less dense, enabling it to absorb and embody ever higher levels of plasma frequency light that our system has been exposed to over this Stellar Activation Cycle. This in turn permits the vibration rate of our particle body to massively accelerate in order to match parallel anti-particle spin and also match the higher frequency bands we are moving into.

In addition to this, the Aurora have been working with the Krystal Star, or Krystal River host races, to rehabilitate and recode damaged planetary grids to ensure the morphogenetic fields of the planet can hold and anchor the Krystal Star frequencies of Kryst or Christos consciousness into the planet.

Once safe they have built what are called Aurora Platforms which are effectively 'safe zones' to enable one's consciousness to 'step over' the damaging and confining reversals fields, frequency fences and NETs[23]. This gives our consciousness safe access to where we need to go in the next stage of the Ascension journey.

---

[23] Nibiruian Electrostatic Transduction fields – see Appendix C

I liken the Aurora Platforms to rather like throwing a blanket over some barbed wire so we can safely step over without getting snagged. We first encounter these platforms usually through meditation practice as we find we can 'glide' or 'slide' a portion of our consciousness onto these platforms, before moving out further into our universe and beyond.

Those with the ability, and who wish to, can also take a portion of their body, their etheric body, on this journey of exploration so we can go adventuring in a way that has been denied to us for a very long time.

The Aurora races, or Aurora Host as they are being called have also undertaken to act as the Host Matrix for the coming period of evolution for humanity. They took over this role from the Melchizedeks, who have been the genetic hosting race of the earth's ascension cycle for the last 35,000 years, but have themselves suffered damage and digression due to what has occurred here.

We owe a great debt of gratitude to both the Aurora and the Krystal Star or River races for the powerful and essential help they have been providing to us, and the tireless efforts they have put into ensure that this Ascension cycle is successful.

Bifurcation of Timelines

I talked briefly in the introduction about the 'split' or bifurcation of timelines that had occurred, and want to expand on that a little further here.

As I talked about in the introduction it was a point of no return where Fallen races began to journey forwards on the essentially destructive path of the Fibonacci current of universal energy, whilst all ascending races, including those of Earth who are committed to Ascension, even if unconsciously, began to move forward on the organic infinite energy currents of the Krystal spiral.

One group is set on an ascending path to ever higher frequencies, whilst the other will stay within the low frequency realms and move into whatever future they are creating for themselves. Effectively there is a group which are tuning in and connecting to 5th dimensional consciousness and its resulting morphogenetic blueprint, and another group which is quite simply not! They are sticking with the 3D blueprint and not budging.

The bifurcation of time into the two different timelines is playing out and becoming ever more obvious right now. The last couple of years in particular has seen an increasing level of intensity, seeming chaos and polarity amplification which we have all had to find ways of coping with (or not!).

Our own integrity and mastery of energetic fields is being tested, and whilst the collective mind of humanity is going through a dark night of the soul experience as the sifting and sorting and splitting apart is underway it is **how we deal with this** that is the real test. None of us are exempt from the chaos, breakdown, confusion, uncertainty and stress that is playing out around us, but we can choose to observe this calmly and maintain our frequency and

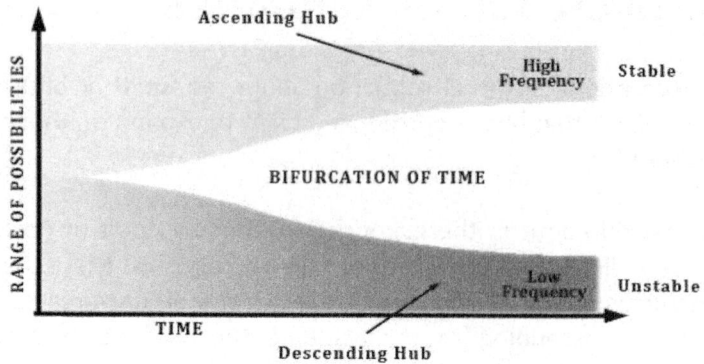

upward path, or we can choose to descend into the drama becoming part of the problem.

Adaptability, flexibility, neutrality and the ability to take the eagle's eye view on what is playing out are the skills that need to be adopted and fostered. Personally speaking, I have had to shift from someone who wanted everything planned out well in advance to being able to shift and change plans and focus in a heartbeat. It was a difficult process to start with, but once I decided to play with it, and just have some fun, it became so much easier, and I now love not knowing what is going to happen from one moment to the next. It is huge fun and very liberating and full of surprises.

There are a couple of things worth noting here. One is that the group moving into the 5D blueprint are also shifting from the Lunar Matrix[24] and its distortions, installed in the lower 3D, which essentially has a set of zodiacal calendar positons installed within the 3D Cosmic Clock (Fallen consciousness controlled) into the 5D Solar Matrix zodiacal calendar positions.

---

[24] The Lunar Matrix was generated by the Fallen races to suppress, distort and influence human consciousness into their desired pathways

Sign	Dates	Alchemical Theme	Element
♈ Aries	Apr 19 - May 13	Purification, Calcination	Fire
♉ Taurus	May 14 - Jun 19	Congelation, Transformation	Earth
♊ Gemini	Jun 20 - Jul 20	Fixation, Synthesis	Air
♋ Cancer	Jul 21 - Aug 9	Dissolution, Dismantling	Water
♌ Leo	Aug 10 - Sep 15	Digestion, Conversion	Fire
♍ Virgo	Sep 16 - Oct 30	Distillation, Purity	Earth
♎ Libra	Oct 31 - Nov 22	Sublimation, Transmutation	Air
♏ Scorpio	Nov 23 - Nov 29	Separation, Stillness	Water
⛎ Ophiuchus	Nov 30 - Dec 17	Unification, Wound Healing	Water/Aether
♐ Sagittarius	Dec 18 - Jan 18	Incineration, Resurrection	Fire
♑ Capricorn	Jan 19 - Feb 15	Fermentation, Illumination	Earth
♒ Aquarius	Feb 16 - Mar 11	Multiplication, Virtues	Air
♓ Pisces	Mar 12 - Apr 18	Ascension, Perfection, Christos-Sophia	Water/Aether

This process has been gradual and began around 10 years ago, and has required many upgrades and corrections in order to activate the corrected Solar Zodiac imprints, and this was fully completed finally in 2023. It was a very clear marker of the forward trajectory of this ascending timeline. Not only does it return us to the ancient galactic zodiac imprints but is moving us once more back into a zodiac which recognises 13 signs.

The constellation of Ophiuchus is the 13th constellation which has been missing whilst humanity has been buried in the imposed Lunar Matrix. It will be interesting to see when astrologers begin to pick this us. It will also be interesting to note if Sideral Astrology[25], rather than the more prevalent Tropical Astrology also begins to come to the fore.

This change will mean that the magnetic imprint received by each individual as they birth on Earth will change for those currently being born, whilst those of us somewhat longer in the tooth may

---

[25] Tropical astrology fixes the constellations in a pattern that is astronomically incorrect and now, I understand, over 2,000 years out of date, whereas Sideral astrology is based on where the constellations are at this current moment.

find that our birthchart does not have the same resonance, nor the same influence on our body, personality and mind in the years ahead.

Another important effect that many will have noticed already is what I call 'Instant Karma'. Karma relates to the Universal Law of Cause and Effect[26]. Within the next Harmonic Universe (HU2), the frequency is higher, therefore faster moving, and this will have the effect of manifesting the consequences of the Law of Cause and Effect much more quickly. Rather than waiting often the best part of a lifetime, or even until the next lifetime, for the consequences to return to us, it will be much more immediate, sometimes within days.

What we energetically send out will return to us, as it always has done, only much faster. It will also be a more accurate frequency match also, so the higher you keep your own personal frequency the better the results from the actions you take, providing they are in Service-to-Others.

It is a very simple understanding really, and karma will become a lot more 'real' to us as a concept when we see the effects of our actions materialise much quicker and more effectively before us. So the quality of our thoughts, beliefs, behaviours, emotions and actions is likely to become ever more apparent to us, reflected in what plays out around us, making it easier to see where we still have work to do to master things at these levels.

The higher timeline we are shifting to is essentially the Christos/Krystic Law of One timeline.

---

[26] See my book The Universal Laws

Christos Law of One Teachings

The Law of One, also called the Christos Teachings and the Essene or Nazarene Teachings, recognises the Universal Truth that All is One – a truth that still echoes through many of our ancient spiritual teachings, and is recognised as Unity Consciousness. It contains within it the awareness that we all come from the same Source and are all part of this Source, no matter our shape, size, colour, point of origin etc. Every living entity is connected and part of the whole due to this simple fact.

Furthermore it recognises that everything is made up of intelligent energy that we call consciousness, and that this consciousness is both from Source and *is* Source.

When properly recognised and understood this is a very powerful and unifying force. Love, the frequency of Love is the organic consciousness of God/Source/Creator or whatever word you wish to use. This energy pervades all Creation, all beings, and unites us all. We simply have to recognise this and work to embody this. It is the unifying and overarching energy of this Universe, and is the beating heart of the Christos teachings.

Each being who is committed to the Law of One seeks to embody this unity principle, to practice loving kindness and compassion and embody the understanding that what you do to one, ultimately you do to all, including oneself.

It seeks to recognise that each being, each spark of consciousness that is the Divine incarnate, is on its own journey of experience, is evolving along its own path. Each soul evolves in its own time and all are at different levels, but that is ok and as it should be. Each will follow different timelines and participate in different holographic realities, and that too is as it should be.

None are more elevated than another, 'special or chosen'. All have equal value, all are interconnected and all are interdependent.

None sits above another regardless of where they are in their ascension journey – indeed a more evolved being has a responsibility to help one who is less evolved to find their way. By living in awareness of this understanding, by living in accordance with these teachings that express unconditional Love to all Creation, it brings us into a state of unity with the energy of Source or Universal Consciousness.

Furthermore we should act and behave in a way that we would desire that others do so towards us. It is a simple thing really but so many fail to see that the way they behave would outrage them if they were on the receiving end.

By adhering to these very simple principles it can bring us into a high state of expanded consciousness and frequency that unifies and leads us to spiritual freedom.

The Law of One has been the founding principle of our universe or Time Matrix since it was created around 950 billion years ago. It is a unifying principle for all races across the galaxy, excepting those Fallen Races whose templating digressed to the extent they chose to detach from these unifying principles in order to follow their own agendas of aggression, domination, control and destruction.

The Law of One was gifted to humanity at its original seeding here on Earth via what are called the Emerald Founder Records or the Cloister Dora-Teura (CDT) Holographic Plates. These plates contain not only the teachings of the Law of One, but also the knowledge of the origins, genetics and purpose of the human race, and included also the galactic history of this Time Matrix which is the birthright of all Angelic humans. There are 12 plates in all and they were closely guarded and protected. As you can imagine they are highly prized by both Christos and Fallen races alike, and have been the cause of much hunting down and suffering and damage. As a result they are currently off-planet in the safe-keeping of those who gifted them to us, until such time as we are safe once more to take them back into our care.

Practices

There are seven simple practices that make up the Law of One:

The Practice of Unity Consciousness – encapsulated in the saying All is One and embracing the Divine in everything. It is a matter of recognising that not only is humanity all the same under the skin, but all Life is equally worthy.

The Practice of Loving Yourself - we cannot truly love others if we do not love ourselves. By loving, honouring and respecting oneself we are acknowledging the Divine with us and embodying the Divine energy of Love within us. It is an act of Self Sovereignty.

The Practice of Loving Others – by learning to love ourselves, we learn to love others and see within them the same Divine energy which is within us. Hold others in the same love, respect and honour that you hold yourself, and have compassion and non-judgment for all, for we are all on unique paths and all are of equal value.

The Practice of Loving Earth and Nature – Divine Consciousness is alive within all things. Our Mother Earth and all her creations, all her kingdoms of plants, animals, minerals and all the unseen kingdoms of nature spirits, all are part of the Divine and all contain Divine consciousness to be held in Love, respect and honour. This brings harmony to the way in which we co-exist with our close neighbours, the different plant, animal, mineral and elemental kingdoms, and the planet.

The Practice of Service to Others – find ways in which you can help serve others individually and also the Collective. This is not a case of overstepping personal boundaries, nor is it about egoic entitlement or attachment. It is a quiet, humble practice without expectation that is part of a flow of energy exchange which expands and extends the field of consciousness. It could simply be called being neighbourly.

The Practice of Consciousness Expansion – this is a process of consciousness embodiment and recognition of the spiritual identity. If the ego still has any kind of authority it will block this from happening, and it requires discipline and awareness of the mind and thoughts and the ability to sit in patience and wait for the mind to quiet in order to listen to inner spirit and guidance. This in turn will lead you where you need to go to expand your awareness and consciousness into a gnosis of the sovereignty and unity of all things free from fear and dogma.

The Practice of Responsible Co-Creatorship – as consciousness expands and activates ever greater levels of our DNA templating we become more aware of our Divine purpose of being a co-creator with God. We share a unity of purpose and direction and seek to live in a way which totally embodies this. Nothing is done from ego, but from the gnosis, or inner knowing, of unity consciousness and that we do not control, possess or know better than anything or anyone else. We therefore do not impose our will, but seek to express the Divine energy of Love which flows through us to all Creation.

Remember also that there are many paths that lead back to Source. None are better than any other, all have equal value, and each being's journey is unique. All comes from Source and all should be used to honour and serve the Divine in Creation.

It is also worth noting that your spiritual practice should feel right for you – it should be your own, not imposed on you, so leave anything that does not feel right for you at this time.

Be aware that some may wish to come together under a common heading, whilst others may wish to remain private in their practice. All that is required is to recognise the divinity in both yourself and others and in all Creation, no matter what you call it.

By putting our focus on Other rather than Self we expand our awareness and therefore our spiritual power and effectiveness out into the world.

Note: This is NOT the same as the Ra Material The Law of One (also called the Book of War) which is 'channelled' from the Anunnaki entity Marduke of the Marduke-Luciferian Anunnaki.

Summary

Throughout the book I have talked about the various things we need to do that are part of the Ascension process but I want to finish by bringing together in one place the different practices and things that are encompassed in the Sacred Science of Ascension.

It is a practice and a way of being in the world, of embodying certain principles and frequencies, and surrendering to the flows of energy that carry you forward on the path laid out. It may appear fairly simple and straightforward as an undertaking, but is not easy. It requires strength, determination and commitment. Often simple things require great discipline and staying power to achieve, and there are no short-cuts. If anyone is offering you shortcuts, it is likely they are appealing to your lower self and you will not achieve your goals.

Stick to the work, however, and the reward is well worth the effort. I can't stress that highly enough!

Becoming Conscious and Aware
Whilst, at a Soul or Higher Self, level we may be committed to follow the ascending path, it is not until we consciously connect that we can begin the first step on the road to mastery.

Also called awakening, this often is a process that unfolds over a period of time where we become aware that there is more to life than simply working, playing and buying 'stuff'. We actively start seeking 'something more'.

This is where there is much exploration of ancient teachings, different spiritual offerings, various New Age modalities and so on. There will also be a growing desire to connect more into Nature and its ancient natural cycles, and come back into alignment with natural rhythms.

Know Yourself
As part of the ongoing process of becoming more conscious we have to begin to drop the personality overlays and facades that most of us adopt in order to 'fit in' or project the right kind of persona for the people we are around. Instead we have to come back into alignment with our true Self, our true personality at the 3-D level.

For some this is simple, for many this is very difficult as they have been taught to be otherwise in order to be accepted. I found this part very difficult, as I had hidden myself within the persona of the people pleaser, having learnt from an early age that if I wasn't to draw down criticism and disapproval this was what I had to do. It is often a defensive measure we adopt as children that we then become 'stuck' in.

There are many ways to begin to reclaim yourself. Questions such as 'What do I *really* like?' 'What makes my Soul sing?' ' Where are my beliefs/behaviour adopted from those around me, and not my own at a deeply held and sincere level?' 'Which parts of me are inauthentic?' all need answering.

Various forms of self-development are helpful here, and each has something to offer.

Shadow Work
This is where the process really begins in earnest. What we mean when we refer to shadow work is looking at all those aspects of Self we find unacceptable, not so nice or not quite good enough for some mythical standard we hold ourselves to. This can also be where we hold onto old angst, emotional wounds, grudges, resentments and such like, all of which cause blockages in the free flow of energy within our lightbody, and can cause great problems if not released.

This is often referred to as the purification and healing stage as we address old traumas and limiting beliefs and begin the first step towards releasing the ego's hold. Depending upon what skeletons lie buried in your cupboard it can be a painful time, as we face and accept those aspects of ourselves we dislike and revisit and let go of many painful memories and hurts.

It is challenging but necessary work. There is a saying 'the challenge becomes the gift', referring to the spiritual gold that lies in doing this work. It is true alchemy, turning the heavy lead of the personality self into the spiritual gold of the Soul.

At the same time as engaging with all of this, meditation practices, energy work and therapies and working intentionally to open yourself to higher realms and levels of being can all be of help.

A lot of the above is about clearing and letting go of heavier frequencies held within the body and lightbody, so energy flows freely and any problem areas that arise are quickly addressed. Much as a hot air balloon sheds ballast in order to rise, we must do the same to begin to align ourselves with the higher frequency fields.

Do not be surprised if you fall in and out of these fields initially. By sticking with what you are doing and not being discouraged when there is a backward step you will find yourself beginning to naturally inhabit the higher fields for longer and longer, until that is where most of your time is passed. Resilience and determination will get you there.

Integration and Embodiment
This is an ongoing process, as once we have dropped the 'weight' in whatever form it may appear, we have to integrate and embody the higher frequency fields we can inhabit. We begin to live the truth we have discovered, and our perception and understanding of the world around us – and ourselves - begins to change into something much more wondrous little by little.

This in turn leads us into a deeper connection to Source and our Divine Spark. We begin to focus more fully (and better understand the implications of) the Christos teachings.

Transcendence
Slowly but surely the move into alignment with the Self, and moving beyond duality and fear becomes embedded, until you are viewing the outside world from an Observer stance. Your sense of connection to all Life deepens and expands until you KNOW yourself and the universe and all in it are One.

Your Checklist

- Learn to love and accept yourself, warts and all.
- Let go of all negative emotions, beliefs and behaviours that block your growth.
- Treat others as you would wish to be treated – be neighbourly.
- Be kind in all your dealings with yourself and others.
- Learn to master your emotions and thoughts so you are not triggered by outside influences.
- Study and understand the Universal Laws, and mechanics of how energy works – particularly pay attention to the Law of Cause and Effect and how that is playing out in your life.
- Reconnect to Nature and natural rhythms and cycles.
- Honour all life equally.

- Hold personal honour high – be good for your word. If you make a commitment, keep it. It erodes your sovereignty if you commit to something and do not follow through. This is about building a back-bone and not a wish-bone.
- Study and work with practices that expand consciousness and enable embodiment of higher frequency harmonics.
- Maintain good lightbody hygiene – ensure you build energetic layers of protection to keep yourself free from outside interference and corruption.
- Recognise when your ego is still in charge and may be running the show.
- Cultivate the ability to surrender to your highest potential and Source. Thy will not my will, or as I like to say 'Let go, and let God'.
- Become aware of the light you hold within you, and anchor it wherever you go. Light is frequency, and your field will affect others.

Ultimately, this process is the reason you incarnated here. The true work is to re-activate and heal back into alignment with your original organic DNA template. It may seem, at times, like parts of this work are very esoteric, but your True Self, the divine cosmic light being who is you, know what it is doing.

All 'little you' has to do is surrender and align to the process and commit to doing what is required.

Appendices

Appendix A
The Difference Between Fibonacci v Krystal Spirals

Gaining an understanding of the difference between the death mechanics of the Fibonacci Spiral, which gives us the Golden Mean, and the eternal Krystal Spiral is probably one of the most fundamental ways of understanding exactly how the artificially created version of 'reality' which we have inhabited for thousands of years, has distorted the true creational blueprint, and how deep into every aspect of our lives and the world around us it has penetrated.

Before we go any further though I want to say that since 2012 this hijack of the Fibonacci spiral math sequencing into the creational currents into our universe, our solar system and our own templating has been released, and the geometries of the Krystal spiral architecture are in the process of re-establishing themselves within the many galactic, planetary and personal fields. This is a MASSIVE change and is fundamental to all the changes occurring currently.

Here we are going to look at the differences between each of these creational spirals and how one is an artificial life current and the other an eternal one.

Let's start by understanding the basic sequencing of each of

```
0, 1, 1                              0, 1
0, 1, 1, 2                           0, 1, 1
0, 1, 1, 2, 3                        0, 1, 1, 2
0, 1, 1, 2, 3, 5                     0, 1, 1, 2, 4
0, 1, 1, 2, 3, 5, 8                  0, 1, 1, 2, 4, 8
0, 1, 1, 2, 3, 5, 8, 13              0, 1, 1, 2, 4, 8, 16
0, 1, 1, 2, 3, 5, 8, 13, 21          0, 1, 1, 2, 4, 8, 16, 32
0, 1, 1, 2, 3, 5, 8, 13, 21, 34      0, 1, 1, 2, 4, 8, 16, 32, 64
0, 1, 1, 2, 3, 5, 8, 13, 21, 34, 55  0, 1, 1, 2, 4, 8, 16, 32, 64, 128
                                     0, 1, 1, 2, 4, 8, 16, 32, 64, 128, 256
```

these. On the left you have the **Fibonacci** sequence of growth, and the on the right the **Krystal** sequencing.

Many of you will be familiar with the Fibonacci spiral and its sequencing of numbers as it is cited often in sacred geometry and in the many ways it shows up in nature. The numbers are obtained by adding the first two numbers together, and then adding the next two and so on. BUT it is only the last 2 digits in the sequence the whole time, ignoring those that came before. So 0 +1 = 1, 1 + 1 = 2, 1 + 2 = 3, 2 + 3 = 5 and so on.

The Krystal Spiral on the other hand adds together ALL the preceding numbers in the table in order to move the sequence forwards. It begins with 0, then 1, then 0 +1 = 1, then 0 + 1 + 1 = 2, then 0 + 1 + 1 +2 = 4 and so on.

So, at first glance the Fibonacci only ever utilises the last two preceding numbers, whilst the Krystal sequence utilises ALL the preceding numbers.

The Fibonacci sequence consumes or eliminates all but two of the numbers that came before in order to grow.

The Krystal sequence grows by including all of the numbers that came before.

One eliminates, the other includes. When we look at this from the movement of energy of consciousness we begin to understand how very different the outcomes of these two spirals are.

The Fibonacci spiral builds and expands by adding together the last 2 numbers, and very quickly loses its connection to its beginning or start point of zero. If you replace the word zero with Source you may begin to see what I am getting at. As it loses its connection with Source it has to climb on the shoulders as it were, of the preceding number to expand and go further. There is no centre point of connection for it to return to, or to which it is connected to carry it forwards or draw on. It has to use the resources around it to expand. To state it more clearly, it attaches to another living organism or entity and uses the energy of this in order to grow and expand.

The Krystal Spiral on the other hand *always* retains it connection to Source, as it unfurls from the centre point or 0, and maintains its connection with EVERY number/being/entity in the sequence. It is continuously fed energy to expand ever outwards by all that has gone before.

Gives a whole new understanding to 'All is One' doesn't it?

There is so much esoteric understanding which begins to unpack from this.

What the Fibonacci Spiral Tells Us

The Fibonacci Spiral demonstrates a predatorial and parasitical behaviour to maintain growth and expansion and all that is created from it. Within the galactic planes it is referred to as the Demon Seed ratio, because as it grows and expands it is only due to the fact it has consumed the previous values in order to do so. It is this basic geometry that spawns the Beast Machine and its artificial demon seed creations or entities, which feed upon living systems in order to survive. This is the true sign of the Beast.

It is from these currents that the Artificial Tree of Life, Metatronic Reversal grids, and the consumptive modelling behaviours we are all so familiar with have sourced.

The fact that the Fibonacci sequencing and spiral are found encoded within natural forms on Earth tells us that this geometry has been programmed into the field architecture of the Earth and infests everything that inhabits the Earth.

All physical form that has this sequencing has a finite nature as its growth pattern inevitably disconnected it from its eternal Source energy, resulting in a recycling of finite energy within this closed system until it has consumed itself ie. a finite life cycle and inbuilt deterioration and ageing until death occurs. Without its Source connection the form is disconnected from the life current that energetically feeds it, with obvious consequences.

We see this patterning programmed into the artificial grids which have been installed on the Earth, overlaying the organic consciousness grids and warping and siphoning their energy into the overlays, which are used to feed the biological parasites which rely on this to sustain their illusion of 'immortality'.

Another name you may see for this energy patterning is Metatronic reversal – named after a fallen consciousness gestalt called the Metatron – or reversal 55 currents. All refer to the distorting of our original templating from eternal energy flows. You also might hear this referred to not so jokingly as the 'Fib-of-no-chi', referring to the Death Mechanics encoded within it.

The good news is that for those of us who have not chosen to disconnect from Source, our original templating is still intact underneath this artificial overlay and can be redeemed. Therefore if you are thinking you have been damned to finite existence due to having been incarnated on Earth, this is only true if you have chosen to disconnect from Source and throw in your lot with the Fallen races, or your template has lost too much energy to be able to hold form.

What the Krystal Spiral Tells Us
The Krystal Spiral is symmetrical in its expansion, and sequences perfectly for exponential growth. It originates from very close to the centre of creation, and aligns with one's own centre and core energy as it spirals out from here through the various layers and levels.

Due to its unbroken connection to Zero Point or Source it is self-perpetuating and self-sustaining. The expanded consciousness field always remains connected to its origins and is therefore eternal. It may be of interest to know that the human template was not designed to be finite, but immortal and before the

Metatronic Death Star harness of the Fibonacci sequencing was introduced all humans maintained their physical body by ingesting life force from the earth grids.

As a spiral it forms a smooth curve that does not differ, whatever the scale and its architecture is fully supportive of an open living universe maintaining all of its connections to the higher dimensions and domains even from the dense levels we inhabit. This also ensures that the eternal energy form will always remain unique and differentiated, whilst also always having a direct, immediate and permanent connection to its own Source fields.

The Permanent Seed Atom within each form is the centre point for the unfurling of this spiral. Within the human template this is the higher heart or 8th chakra, at the thymus level. This connects into the centre point of the 12-Tree grid template at the 8th point and so on.

To access and activate the Permanent Seed Atom we need to come to a point within our own light bodies where we can heal and merge the split of masculine and feminine energies, bringing them together in sacred union. This activates the Permanent Seed Atom, and as the Krystal Spiral begins to re-establish itself within our template and that of the Earth as more energy becomes available to us to begin to embody this new/original templating and bring with it both a balanced wholeness and understanding of unity consciousness.

The illustrations on the next page help us see both the asymmetry of the Fibonacci spiral and the symmetry of the Krystal spiral, as well as the way the latter unfurls from our own central point of the higher heart.

So you can hopefully begin to see from what I have outlined, how devastating the introduction of the Fibonacci energy spiral has been to both us as a race and also much of our universe.

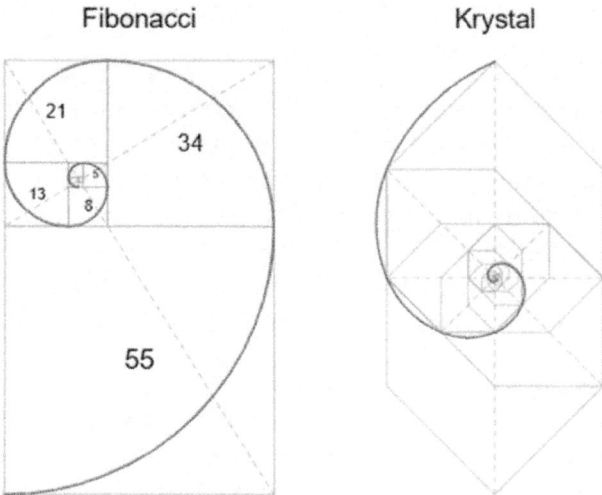

It has been catastrophic to not only our ability to maintain an eternal, living body but has distorted every level of creation it touches.

Many wonder why we talk of this particular moment in Earth's timelines as 'the chance for an evolutionary leap', 'the beginning of a New Age', 'the coming of a Golden Age'.... With the enabling of the return of the Krystic spiral of energy back into our universe, our planet and ourselves at this moment in time, maybe you can begin to get a flavour of what this really means?

Are the Fallen races still here? Yes, some but to an ever-lessening degree. They do not have the DNA template to interfere with the Krystal spiral, or even rise to the higher dimensional levels that the new energies coming to Earth are opening up.

The energetic architectures that are currently being anchored in once more at every level are anathema to them and as Earth accretes more and more Higher Source energy into her fields this will only increase.

Those with this fallen level of consciousness – and their many minions – who still remain on the Earth's surface are desperately promoting their many monstrous programmes of catastrophe, Armageddon, cataclysm, pestilence, war and terrorism trying to claw back lost ground.

All we have to do to ensure they do not pull us into the phantom pit[27] of their making which is the only place they can survive is to focus our attention on the expanding energies, tune into our own God spark connection to the Source fields and let the ever increasing levels of high frequency energy heal and expand this connection, being prepared to embrace the change of templating.

The Krystal energies will do the rest!

---

[27] This refers to the Phantom Matrix, a reversal image of this living Time Matrix, disconnected from Source or life-force energy 'inhabited' by fallen planets and beings needing living, organic systems and beings to feed it.

Appendix B – The CDT Plates

The CDT Plates or Cloister-Dora-Teura Plates are 12 holographic recording, storage and transmission devices gifted to the human race lineage by the Founders Races and contain the full evolutionary history of life within our Time Matrix from 950 billion years ago to the present, as well as extensive educational teachings around Creation Mechanics and advanced Spiritual Teachings.

The Plates were originally manufactured at the Founder's instigation by the Taran Priests of Ur and the Maharaji Sirian-Blue Human Holy Grail Lines races of the Council of Azurline.

In 246,000 BC they were gifted to the Urtite[28] Human Races by the Azurite Races of Sirius B at the first seeding of physical humanity on 3-D Earth in honour of the Urtites entering the Founders Races Emerald Covenant Co-Evolution Agreement.

The CDT Plates hold the ancient records on 12 silver-metallic discs manufactured from a form of striated-selenite-quartz crystal which is organic to the HU2 or 2nd Density planet of Sirius B, surrounding a radioactive isotopic core. This is then overlaid or encased in a hybrid-metal silver-alloy compound which is organic to Earth.

On the gifting of these plates to Urtite Humanity the first written translation was undertaken and became a collection of large books called the Maharata. This was a collection of over 500,000 pages of text transcription held in 590 large embossed leather-bound volumes written on a form of durable textile-paper resembling crisp, semi-translucent vellum.

---

[28] The Urtites were the primary hosting race of the first seeding of the twelve tribes of humanity on the Earth.

The original transcription was in the Anuhazi language, the first spoken and written language of this Time Matrix.

The 12 CDT Plates were kept on Earth until the Urtite human culture was wiped out in 208,216 BC at the time of a failed Stellar Activation Cycle, when there was a deliberate pole shift achieved through machinations and infiltration of Negative Forces wanting to take down the human lineage.

Just prior to this the Sirius B Azurite races retrieved 10 of the 12 CDT Plates and placed them under the protection of the Azurite Universal Templar Security Team.

The CDT Plates are highly coveted by all interstellar races because of the information they contain. But there is also a secondary reason why they are so highly prized. They are part of a large apparatus that includes 12 further silver discs, which are larger than the CDT Plates, called the 12 Signet Shields. Signet refers to Stargate and they are a technology through which the 12 Primary Star Gates of the Universal Templar Complex of this Time Matrix, spanning the densities and dimensions, can be activated.

Between them the 12 CDT Plates can be used to remotely manually activate the Signet Shields and their corresponding Stargates. As Activators of the Signet Shields, in the wrong hands ownership of the CDT Plates could be devastating.

Whilst the Azurites reclaimed 10 of the 12 CDT Plates, 2 of them, and all 12 of the Signet Shields were lost, moving between various competing human and Fallen Angelic Legions on Earth since this time.

In the 1600s the Azurites finally regained possession of one of the missing plates, and in November 1999 the last of them, called the 'Tables of Testimony' by the Knights Templar, was retrieved.

The 12 Signet Shields are currently buried in various secret locations around the Earth.

Since 208,216 BC the Azurites have offered the human race at specific points in the timeline dispensations of knowledge translated from the CDT Plates.

We see these crop up at various times in our history only for the pure teachings to be very quickly – and deliberately – compromised, corrupted, distorted and misrepresented. The Book of Enoch is a case in point, as are the teachings of the Essenes known as John the Baptist and Jesus Christ. The Cathars also held information through genuine Essene records but were exterminated by the Vatican in 1244 AD. Hindu, Chinese, Tibetan, African, Egyptian, Mayan, Incan and Celtic-Druidic lines have all brought through information at various points in these culture's history, only for it all to suffer the same fate of destruction or distortion by the Negative Forces.

Translation of the CDT Plates have been returning to humanity through the auspices of certain individuals at the time of this Stellar Activation Cycle in order to help guide humanity through the process, and helping restore the lost knowledge and understanding of humanity's lineage and purpose to the badly manipulated and mind-controlled population of Earth.[29]

So what information do the CDT Plates contain? Different discs contain certain types of information which when brought together as a whole form a complete Sacred Science.

Amongst the practical physical and spiritual evolutionary advancement teachings is the full evolutionary history of the development of life in our Time Matrix, extensive educational records pertaining to Founders Race Creation Mechanics, Universal Unified Field Physics, Law of One – Inner Christ

---

[29] Please be aware these are not 'channelled' teaching which are often highly suspect. The CDT Plates are holographic in nature and deliver 'downloads' of frequency information which then needs to be 'translated' from its holographic, audio, visual or digital data form by the chosen individuals into our often inadequate languages.

teachings and Ascension-Merkaba training, the history and details of the Emerald Covenant and humanity's historical relationship to this, teachings of Planetary, Galactic and Universal Star Gate mechanics, DNA Template Bio-Regenesis and Kathara Core Template Healing technologies and much more besides.

All of these were gifted to the human race in order to enable Angelic Humanity to fulfil its original 'Creation Commission' as guardians and keepers of the Universal Templar Complex – a purpose we are a long way from currently achieving at the moment.

Amongst the various books which I am aware of are:

The Book of the Dragon
The Book of Amenti
The Angelic Rosters
The Tablets of Testimony
Keylontic Morphogenetic Science
Books of Maps and Key
The Books of Enoch

Emerald Tablets of Thoth the Atlantean

I think it is worth mentioning here what are known as the Emerald Tablets, written by Thoth the Atlantean. These are writings which are said to have formed the basis of Hermeticism, amongst other sacred teachings, given by the Egyptian/Atlantean god Thoth, also known as Hermes or Hermes Trismegistus.

Thoth is from the fallen Sirian-Anunnaki lineage. For many thousands of years he voluntarily took part in the Bio-Regenesis programme, which seeks to correct DNA distortions and return the DNA potential of anyone willing to participate to its full 12-strand potential, even those of Anunnaki origin who willingly disconnected their 12th strand.

Things had gone so well, and Thoth had worked himself into such a place of trust with those running the Bio-Regenesis programmes that he had been granted a certain amount of access to the CDT plates.

In a betrayal which has echoed down the recent historical timeline so horrific were its effects, he turned on the Guardian Alliance, stole CDT Plate 10 and instigated what is called the Eieyani Massacre, one of the more horrific of the Fallen Angelic betrayals.

He wrote the Emerald Tablets as a distorted version of the pure teachings, which have been creating havoc within mystery schools and sacred societies ever since, designed to ensure that well-meaning people were corrupted into enacting fallen, reversal ascension mechanics and having their light siphoned into the dark agendas of the Fallen Races.

So whilst the Emerald Tablets are based on CDT plate 10, they are NOT the pure teachings but a highly corrupted and damaging version.

Appendix C - The NET and Frequency Fences

NET stands for Nibiruian Electrostatic Transduction fields and they were created at the time of last failed Stellar Activation cycle by the Nibiruian Anunnaki, one of the Fallen races causing so much trouble here on Earth.

It was anchored into the Earth using both the Nibiru Diodic Crystal (NDC) grid and the Nibiru Crystal Temple Network[30], two networks created around the same time, all designed to interact and power up various mind control broadcast system.

This 4-D NET effectively enshrouds the Earth by impacting scalar sonic pulses against the Earth's inner grid system and creating an 'interference' pattern or electrostatic force field.

It has the effect of 'quarantining' the Earth from both incoming and outgoing signals to a very large extent from and to the higher dimensions. Thus it prevented Guardian teams from either communicating with their incarnated forces on Earth or maintaining a steady surveillance ability of what was happening on Earth beneath the NET due to its 'cloaking' ability which gave false readings. It effectively cut Earth off from much in the way of help from the Higher Dimensions during this last Dark Age.

In 9,558 BC the 4-D NET was fortified, its ability to block communications strengthened. It is said to be an 'astral mess' (4-D covers the Astral levels) and at this current SAC the Anunnaki

---

[30] 24 subterranean Crystal Temple networks that serve as the main global transmission network of the NDC-grid Checkerboard Matrix control programme and is part of the interstellar Photo-sonic communications system of Earth.

plan, along with their cohorts, is to lower the NET from 4-D to 3-D, tightening the noose on our freedoms and giving them much better control of the population as they seek to impose their One World Order Transhumanist agenda and pull us irretrievably into the Phantom Matrix. We have seen this attempt playing out around us now, but all indications are that despite their best efforts they have failed.

As a consequence of this communications blackout, the NET has enabled Fallen races to control not just our history and collective memory, but also the progress of our science, as they feed us what they want us to know for their own purposes. For example, many electrical technologies have been introduced that will interface with and enable the lowering of the NET from 4-D to 3-D – think wireless technology, electricity grids, HAARP, satellite networks etc.

The NET is effectively a Black Hole technology which turned Earth into a Prison Planet, and ensures that the DNA blocks and damage imposed by the Anunnaki stay in place.

The main operational hub of the NET is in Stonehenge and connects into the Nibiru-Tiamat Phantom Matrix and the full activation of this technology happened during the Atlantian Cataclysm, enabling Fallen Intruder races to install within it hive mind Black Queen entities and their lunar hierarchy, part of the mechanism to destroy the Divine Feminine Sophia consciousness on the planet.

There is a toxic by-product of the NET system, which is an unnatural ozone layer around the planet. This generates interference in how photonic light reaches into the layers of the Earth's atmosphere and along with the current spate of chemtrails it diverts solar plasmic codes that potentially activate dormant human DNA. Fear of the sun and sunlight has also been promoted to the masses, encouraging the use of sun blockers, to prevent this light reaching our cells.

In 1943 via something called the Philadelphia Experiment, which was theoretically a timeshift/invisibility experiment but was in fact manipulated by the Zeta Rigelians[31], one of the competing Fallen races, to enable them to punch holes in the NET in order to provide them with a gateway into Earth space through which they could bring their ships.

This was further expanded in 1983 via a Rigelian-Andromie Alliance, to connect the Phi-Ex Falcon artificial grid to Phantom Alpha & Omega Centauri and Alnitak, Orion, called the Montauk Project, which created the Montauk-Phi-Ex-Falcon artificial grid.

The fall of the Niburuian NET is currently well underway as Guardian teams manoeuvred to gain control over the frequency fences it generates and to also repurpose the Crystal Temple network. In September 2022 it was confirmed that the Black Queen hives had been cleared and gradually the links are falling as other grids are being taken off-line.

Frequency fences refers to mass frequency control devices that have been utilised, (think HAARP, 5G, wireless networks etc) to given the Fallen races increasing levels of power to 'scramble' both selected human brain patterns as well as dull and 'fog up' that of the collective field.

This works to block individuals receiving frequencies coming from outside of the current planetary control network including those coming from other higher dimensional groups of beings who are trying to help our planet in this time of woe, and also frequency patterns emanating from our own personal and collective Soul Matrix.

The energy we identify as sound serves as the 'glue' which holds

---

[31] All Zeta emerge from Zephelium, a tall blue-skinned bipedal insectoid-reptilian-serpent seed race. Zeta Rigelians are an aggressive Omicron hybrid from Rigel, Orion also known as 'Tall Greys'.

together matter patterns in our Time Matrix, so through the manipulation of sound waves many things can be 'created' or influenced at this level. As humans work within a very specific pattern of frequency which directs all body processes and how we perceive our 'reality', the frequency fences put in place a perceptual block by altering the electrical impulse patterns and thus the chemical and hormonal operations within the physical biological body structure which literally creates a barrier against selected electrical impulses or frequencies within the biology.

Amazon Review Request

I hope you have enjoyed the learning and insights *Understanding Ascension* has to offer.

If you are willing to take a moment to go to Amazon and leave a favourable review it would be much appreciated.

This really helps someone like you who wants to know more about **Understanding Ascension** but is unsure where to start and does them a HUGE favour.

My mission is to get this important information to as many people as possible, but to reach more people **I need your help.**

Most people look at the reviews before they buy a book – I know I do! So you would be doing me a HUGE favour *and* helping a fellow traveller on this journey by leaving a review!

It costs nothing, takes only a minute or so and makes a BIG difference.

And is also much appreciated!

Many thanks

Saira

About Saira and Her Work

We all came here for something, and that something wasn't just to go to school, become an employee, pay taxes and die....

Finding out what that something is has been one of the guiding passions of my life as I have dug ever deeper into understanding the many conundrums of life.

A natural researcher and sponge for the many and varied streams of knowledge that have taken my attention over the last 30 years, I have gradually been able to build an insight into the hidden realities of our modern world, its many mysteries, our true origins and purpose and a life-altering understanding of what is playing out around us at this current time.

If you are interested in learning more about the work I do and the information I share you will find much more on my website www.sairasalmon.com. For the latest information and to keep up-to-date join my mailing list.

You can join **The Lost Wisdom Library**, a cornucopia of information from how to treat everyday disease issues with nutrition and herbs to Earth mysteries, our hidden histories, ancient bloodlines and even our galactic histories as well as interviews and insights from some of our great global teachers. It is an ever-growing resource.

Through the **Grail Wisdom** membership group I share more of the concepts, understandings and histories that we should have been taught from birth to understand who we truly are as a race, but which has been denied to us through official channels.

Within **the Life Alchemy** membership groups we explore how we can use this knowledge to deepen our own spiritual journeys and transformation and growth, interacting with the ever-increasing flows of energy surrounding us.

And through the **Guardian Mentorship** programme I work one-to-one with individuals to ensure a more tailored and personal progression.

We are living in pivotal times where so much that had been lost to us is being reclaimed, amidst the extraordinary scenarios currently playing out. Transcending the chaos and working for the highest outcomes for all is not for everyone, but if you feel called, please join me.

I look forward to meeting you

Saira

Acknowledgments

Thanks to Alexander Valchev (Alex_82 on Fiverr) for the cover design.

My thanks also to Lisa Renee of www.energeticsynthesis.com for illustrations on pages 22, 24, 36, 47, 55, 56, 57, 58, 59, 60, 62, 76, 116.

Those on pages 42, 48 are author's own. Any others have come from the vast store I have collected through my research over the years, and have come without attribution. If those from whom they came care to contact me I will correct the oversight.

My thanks also to the many mentors and teachers I have been fortunate enough to meet over the many years I have been doing this work. They are too numerous to mention but know who they are, and all are appreciated for the knowledge, activation and support they have offered to bring me to this place.

Printed in Great Britain
by Amazon